On a Truck Al
to McMahon

On a Truck Alone, to McMahon

NABANEETA DEV SEN

Translated from Bengali by
ARUNAVA SINHA

Edited by
MINI KRISHNAN

For Binky
For now, then, always
Bultu

OXFORD
UNIVERSITY PRESS

OXFORD
UNIVERSITY PRESS

Oxford University Press is a department of the University of Oxford.
It furthers the University's objective of excellence in research, scholarship,
and education by publishing worldwide. Oxford is a registered trademark of
Oxford University Press in the UK and in certain other countries.

Published in India by
Oxford University Press
2/11 Ground Floor, Ansari Road, Daryaganj, New Delhi 110 002, India

First published in Bengali by Ananda Publishers Private Limited in 1984
This English translation published by Oxford University Press India in 2018

ISBN-13 (print edition): 978-0-19-948524-6
ISBN-10 (print edition): 0-19-948524-0

ISBN-13 (eBook): 978-0-19-909372-4
ISBN-10 (eBook): 0-19-909372-5

Typeset in Garamond 3 LT Std 12/15.5
by The Graphics Solution, New Delhi 110 092
Printed in India by Replika Press Pvt. Ltd

Contents

Prologue

Muhurtam jwalitam shreyah
Na tu dhumayitam kroram

Blaze for a moment, rather than smoulder till eternity.
—Vidura to Sanjay, in the Mahabharata

With the taste of salt tea on my tongue, herds of yaks around bends in the mountain road, treeless valleys, unknown plants bare of leaves or flowers, and sunsets minus the warbling of birds, Tawang has been shackled to my heart for five years now, waiting to be written.

What if I cannot draw everyone to my heart and take them all the way to Tawang?

I have no particular objective in life—a thought such as *I hope I can at least accomplish this before I die*. But I cannot be calm. Every moment I launch another paper boat, pushing it away from land with my pen. And then I fret that it might capsize. Even though I know that this boat is not really a boat—it's not going anywhere.

I am so restless.

Now here at home, now there in the world outside. And in my heart? Neither of the two, but eternally on a journey.

Tawang is the story of just such a journey.

Isn't the entire universe accessible to those who are neither in nor outside it?

For as long as I can remember I've been told that I'm wild, uncivilized, eccentric, savage. All right, so be it. Wild animals do have some advantages, don't they, which domestic animals don't. About a hundred domesticated cows swept away into the sea by the floods in Andhra Pradesh had washed up ashore alive. Unable to find their sheds, they wandered into the forest. In a few years they turned into wild beasts. Gathered in packs, shaking their menacing horns, they moved about the forest without caring for human beings.

When people swept away by floods are washed up ashore and brush the sand off their bodies, they too wander into the forest when they cannot find their homes.

Alone.

And reckless.

NABANEETA DEV SEN
February 2018

Taking the Flight

'What are you doing here, Nabaneeta?'

'Going to Jorhat,' I answered, stooping to touch his feet. His hand raised in a gesture of blessing, he said, 'Shibsagar? That's where I'm going to. The Assam Literary Conference, right?'

'Not to Shibsagar, I'm going to Jorhat. This one's only for women. The Assam Women's Literature Conference.'

'We have to take the same flight.'

The location was the lounge of Guwahati Airport, and the time, the last week of October 1977. I had just run into Ashutosh Bhattacharya. Both of us were on our way to security check. We kept chatting during the checks and set off for the plane. Passengers to Jorhat should board now, declared the announcer.

We had stopped for an hour in Guwahati after flying in from Dumdum Airport in Calcutta. A change of plane for Jorhat. Getting to Shibsagar also meant flying to Jorhat. I was delighted to meet Dr Bhattacharya. Who wouldn't be happy to see a familiar face while travelling? He didn't seem displeased either. We took seats next to each other and began to converse happily.

Suddenly I realized that a man was staring fixedly at us from across the aisle. What was this? Why was he staring? Did I know him? No, I didn't. Well then? I realized a little later that it wasn't just him, everyone around us was staring. What a badly behaved plane! Dr Bhattacharya was a white-haired old gentleman of amiable appearance. He could never seem a misfit, no matter whom he was talking to. Why stare at him then? There was no reason to glare at me either. What was it then? Must be something else. Were we talking too loudly? Were we treating the plane like our home? Very politely I said to the first man, 'Sorry, we're very loud, aren't we?' He responded as though he had just found the ground beneath his feet.

'It isn't that, both of you are going to Jorhat, aren't you?'

'Yes,' I answered politely.

'But this plane is going to Calcutta, you see. So, we were wondering....'

'Cal ... cutta?' We shrieked.

'Yes, yes, Calcutta, Calcutta.' The entire plane bellowed at us. 'Get off, get off, wrong plane.'

Ashutosh-babu and I were stupefied.

'But they sent us to this one....'

'No, not this one, there's another one there....Get off, run, it's about to take off....'

We rushed off the plane. Fortunately both of us were carrying nothing but small suitcases. Run, run, run. Dr Bhattacharya could sprint quite fast despite his age. A plane resembling a tiny fish was parked close by, purring like a blissful kitten, the propellers on its nose whirling.

'*Aio*, aio! Is this the plane to Jorhat? Jorhat *jaayga toh?*'

'*Rokke!* Rokke! *Jenana hai!* Stop, lady coming on board!'

With our two separate, distinctive shrieks, we ran breathlessly up to the tiny flying fish. Climbing the short flight of stairs, we found just two seats empty. The plane was packed. Panting, we sat down. At once a smart man in a uniform charged towards us, greeting us with words practically lifted from the poem 'Bonolata Sen'—'Where were you all this time?' His eyes, though, were not birds' nests, but tigers' caves. 'Actually, we got into the wrong plane. A few moments more and we'd have....'

Indeed. What would have happened had those moments passed? Two renowned guests at two literary conferences in Assam. Setting the alarm clock and waking up before dawn with great difficulty to take taxis to the airport, to fly to Guwahati. A few moments more and we would have gone on dignifiedly to land at Dumdum, thinking to ourselves, 'What a big airport Jorhat has! Beats Guwahati hands down.' The very thought made me want to giggle, but out of the corner of my eye, I saw that Dr Bhattacharya was not amused. He was looking grim. Imagine landing back in Dumdum after all the security checks and weighing of luggage and change of aircraft. Ashutosh-babu must have been telling himself, 'This woman is the root of all trouble. Chatters on and on. That's why this happened.' This is true. I am perpetually distracted, and get myself into all kinds of scrapes constantly. Dr Bhattacharya must never have faced such a situation in his life, for these things do not happen to gentlemen. It was only because I was with him that....

My heart beamed as soon as we got off at Jorhat Airport. Hundreds of butterfly clusters in light yellow and white *Begum Bahar* saris flew about in the tall, dense green grass. A different breed of butterflies in gorgeous black and orange *Kanjeevaram* saris were circling over them. This was our welcome committee. Gorgeous! The empty aerodrome was a huge sheet of silver brocade. Glittering in the sunlight, like the forecourt of a rice mill. Green borders of dense grass spangled with birds and butterflies. And not just large butterflies either.

Tiny black-and-brown birds, just like little honey-sucking sunbirds, danced amidst the grass like dragonflies playing hide-and-seek, bickering noisily as they played. And now, at the end of October, in the middle of the day, an ignorant cuckoo (who has no idea how to behave in different seasons) was singing at the top of his voice. Perhaps it had been made a member of the welcoming committee too, and was saying, 'Welcome, Ashu-babu! Welcome, Nabaneeta!'

A tent had been pitched beside the field. Not just any old tent, but a luxurious affair, with chairs and tables, sofas and couches, and a rug. It was like visiting the land of the Bedouins. The chairs were full of people, and the floor, of luggage. Our suitcases were deposited too. The bus would arrive in due course to transport us to the city. Until then, this was our address. This tent, these clusters of butterflies, these flocks of birds, the music of this grass, the sunlight, and the silent music of the glittering dry cement surface.

My throat was parched. Was there no water anywhere in the tent? No, there wasn't. Maybe this really was the land of the Bedouins. When would we go to the city?

~

The Book of the Gathering

The Circuit House in Jorhat was picturesque. Just that one had to cross the drain at the entrance by stepping across thin rods. Walking on them wasn't easy, unless one had shoes as wide as Goodyear or Dunlop tyres. I don't use stilettos or pencil heels, which meant reduced chances of slipping, but I was still apprehensive. Of course, the arrangement was not so much to block women in stilettos as it was to discourage cows, so that they could not wander into the garden for lunch. That was where I met the musical genius Salil Chowdhury for the first time. He too was staying at the Circuit House.

Nirmalprabha Bordoloi and I had been billeted in a room on the first floor. Nirmalprabha had a doctorate in Sanskrit, taught at the Gauhati University, and was a renowned poet. I had already translated some of her lyric poetry. Her verses were often sung. I observed this new aspect of women poets in Assam. They were poets-cum-singers. And scholars too. Dr Lakshahira Das was also a professor at Gauhati University, a poet, and, like Nirmalprabha, a well-known singer. Like Salil Chowdhury, both of them set their own lyrics to tune and went on to sing them too. The songs promptly became hits. Many women poets were present, among them, Neelima Dutt, who also taught at the university. She was a Bengali, but she wrote in Assamese. Her eighteen-year-old son had fallen victim to Naxal politics—Neelima-di's volume of poetry was dedicated to him.

I had already been acquainted with the tremendous power of Nirmalprabha's lines. We had met earlier, in Calcutta. Sharing a room here gave us the chance to become friends, and we chatted all night instead of sleeping. Who would believe that this young poet herself had a daughter who was also a young woman, who also had a PhD, who was also a teacher and a mother! Nirmalprabha's life was the stuff of legends. The more I heard, the more astonished I was. She said that she would dedicate her next book of love poems to a young Bengali poet. And so she did, to Sunil Gangopadhyay.

Besides Nirmalprabha, this was my first exposure to the poetry of many of the other participants. I had no idea that there were so many women poets in Assam. The little magazines from which I had translated poetry did not feature too many women writers. My translations of most Assamese poets had been done with my scanty knowledge of the language and the help of others. Nirmalprabha, Lakshahira, Nabakanta Barua, Hiren Gohanchi, Hiren Bhattacharya, Homen Bargohanchi ... all of them spoke near-fluent Bengali. Refined pronunciation, robust linguistic sense. My Assamese, picked up from reading, was quite raw. Even if I could struggle my way through a book, I could neither speak the language nor write it. No abilities, but a strong yearning—I was greedy for a share of the wealth of Assamese literature.

I said, with great regret in my speech, 'Yes, it is a matter of utmost shame that while we don't even think of inviting Oriya, Hindi, or Assamese writers to Bengali literary conferences, you have done just that. We are callous about these literatures. Neither do we follow them regularly nor do we know the languages, even though there is no lack of Hindi-speaking, Oriya-speaking, and Assamese-speaking people in Calcutta. Yet, living in Assam, you read Bengali literature with such wonderful neighbourly zeal. I am an Assam-lover, though, having learnt a smattering of Assamese in order to read the books *Tomaile* and *Lohitparer Katha* by your poet Amalendu Guha—a Bengali by birth—after which I read some other Assamese poets as well and even translated some of their works. But today when I see your love and respect for Bengali literature, I feel both embarrassed and guilty. It is true that when it comes to literature, Bengalis have remained self-absorbed, under the impression that they are completely self-sufficient. That is why the way your faces light up when you hear names like Ashapurna Devi or Samaresh Basu, Sunil Gangopadhyay or Shakti Chattopadhyay, is not reflected in our case when it comes to your writers. But it is a matter of joy that young writers from little magazines are becoming increasingly conscious of this flaw and are trying to correct it. Many of the smaller journals now have sections devoted to literature from the neighbours. Therefore, the signs are propitious.'

(The literatures of the neighbouring states were discussed soon afterwards in the literary number of *Desh* magazine.) I was fortunate that, possibly because there was no lack of candour in my speech (and definitely because it wasn't very long), everyone was very pleased with it. I am not particularly eloquent, and the appropriate phrase usually refuses to spring to my lips, even though I am given to being a chatterbox. The worst combination, if you know what I mean.

In fact, the respected chief guest was a wondrous example of how to be irreverent without being eloquent. Still, the lady managed to deliver her weighty speech. In fact, a couple of journalists even pursued me to the Circuit House to conduct interviews, looking extremely grave all the while. The first was P.K. Bardoloi, known to everyone as a journalist of the arts, who wrote under the pen name of Aghori. The other one was a young radio journalist. A long interview with Aghori was published in the *Dainik Janmabhoomi*. Aghori sent me a clipping later. I was told that the radio interview would be broadcast from All India Radio, Guwahati. But I did not remember to tune in, because I had already disappeared from Jorhat by then. For, my next journey had begun already. The sisters Niti Baruah and Rani Hendrique, both of them my new Assamese friends, had lovingly taken me to the Kaziranga Forest, simply because I wanted to visit the jungle. How wonderful that forest sojourn was!

~

The Book of the Forest

'I'm not coming for your conference unless you take me to the Kaziranga Forest.' That was my syrupy threat to Sheela Barthakur on the phone when she invited me. She kept her word and packed me off to Kaziranga with friends. Instead of booking me into the tourist lodge, they took me to a marvellous sanctuary. Kamrup Complex. I am yet to come across anything comparable to it anywhere in India. I haven't seen such a wonderful set-up outside the US. There were arrangements for parking, and different options for boarding, depending on your taste.

I took a single hut—I had always dreamt of living in one—at the edge of the hermitage, on the bank of the narrow river. The Kaziranga Forest began across the stream, while on this bank there was a straggling line of houses, running along the main motorable road. The river was narrow, but its currents were swift. A genuine daughter of the Brahmaputra. Her waters rose and fell according to her own will, flooding the banks. A powerful influence. Rivers like these have unique temperaments.

Kamrup Complex was the fruition of the dream of an evergreen ex-journalist named Jagdish Phukan. He had given up his job to move with his wife and children here on the banks of a river at the edge of a jungle, far from human habitation, to conduct his grand experiment on a large plot of land. To foreigners with delicate tastes, he served meat and rice stuffed in bamboo pipes, roasted on an open fire, along with Adivasi liquor in bamboo tumblers, while for brown sahibs he set up candlelit dinners of French cuisine and European wines laid out on lace tablecloths. They ran a magnificent restaurant. I was genuinely astonished. I have not seen another family business in India that is so wonderful, so well-planned (and imaginative), and so artistic.

The hut chosen for me had mud floors, whitewashed mud walls, and a thatched roof, but the bathroom was a concrete and cement structure with Western facilities. There was a small veranda, Indian style, in front of the hut, where one could easily stretch out on a deckchair. The room was furnished with immaculately clean beds and bed linen, a desk and chair, a pitcher of water with a glass, and even English magazines. Candles, a torch, matches, a lantern—all kinds of lights were provided. Even a handheld fan. Oh, if only I could spend my entire life in a room like this! There was no dearth of worldly comforts here. But it suddenly occurred to me—considering the floor and walls were earthen, what if a snake were to emerge from a hole? I'm a Calcutta girl, never learnt how to tackle a snake. Not that I'm claiming to have learnt how to tackle all these ferocious four-legged tigers or lions either. Of course, all you need to do to combat all these foes, so to speak, is to lock all the doors and windows carefully. But snakes?

It's true that snakes were often killed under the *bakul* tree in the yard of our house, Pratichi, in Santiniketan, but I couldn't claim any credit for those acts. And this was a jungle in Assam! No matter what the poet Satyen Dutta might say, bragging about the daring spirit of Bengal, I really don't dance on the head of a snake. That's purely Keshtothakur's territory. I have my handheld fan, my mosquito net, my deckchair. If

I string the net up carefully and huddle beneath it with the fan, I should be safe till morning. But first, some time on the deckchair in the veranda.

It was a beautiful night. Jagdish Phukan, his wife Mira, and daughter Mita were all very pleasant company. Mira looked after the cooking, maintained the rooms, and ran the restaurant, managing the household single-handedly and superbly. Jagdish took care of the machinery, the finances, and everything to do with the bar, along with the garden, the land, and the farming. Mita's formal name was Arghyaa. She helped both her parents. A united, hard-working, educated family with fine sensibilities. Mira was still amazingly young, and so was Jagdish. Their daughter was in college, while their son had recently moved to Calcutta as a junior executive in a tea company. Mother and daughter appeared to be sisters. The creator had given them an abundance of both talent and grace. Jagdish loved poetry—English, Bengali, Assamese.

What was left of the day passed in looking at Jagdish's orchid collection, farms, and garden. They had built a glorious life for themselves; it made me envious. There were several cars to take them to the city and back. They had guns too. There was no question of shooting animals in the forest, but if the animals suddenly invaded their home, they would have to take the law into their hands, wouldn't they?

We decided to visit the forest next morning. Arghyaa would come too, and we would travel on elephant back. The main objective was to view rhinos—deer and tigers and suchlike were extras.

~

The Book of Kaziranga

The Phukans' car dropped us at the forest office. We set off with a guide, Babar Ali. First, we had to cross the river, which we did in a dinghy, rowed by the guide himself. A young boy also came along to take the dinghy back, leaving as soon as we got off. Now it was just the forest, Arghyaa, Babar Ali, and I. Babar Ali was a jovial young man. He helped us up the steep river bank. A dense green forest of tall trees lay ahead, bushes and shrubs with creepers winding around them, exactly the way we imagine a tropical forest. But that was not all there was to Kaziranga. Only a little bit of what I saw was like this. The rest was a swamp filled with tall grass. A small clearing had been created inside the dense jungle. And who was that kneeling on the grass? Mansingh. An enormous tusker, though one of his tusks was missing. Babar Ali propped a ladder up against the elephant, which Arghyaa and I climbed to perch on his back. Babar Ali was the mahout. In other words, he was our friend, philosopher, and guide on this forest trail. He looked less than thirty, a happy-go-lucky lad, whom Arghyaa knew. The forest department had just a handful of regular mahouts on its roster. As soon as Mansingh, Esquire, stood up—how majestic! All the branches and leaves on the tall trees were within my reach now. The green in this forest seemed different, a fresh coat of paint that would rub off on my skin.

Mansingh was indeed an eminent figure, standing tall among elephants. About ten years ago Dhritikanta Lahiri Chowdhury had given me an exhaustive discourse on the different kinds of elephants in Assam. Using colour transparencies at his lectures, he had tried to present all his friends as pachyderm pundits. But now that it was time to apply all that knowledge, I discovered I had forgotten everything. What was the structure of this elephant's back? What about the formation of its feet? The nature of its teeth? The forehead? The tail? Despite my best efforts I could remember nothing, otherwise I could have impressed the mahout. No such luck. The mahout began to impress us instead. This jungle was the one book he had read since birth. He was capable of spouting endless wisdom about it. There was not a question I could ask that he did not have the answer to. Of course, he could have been bluffing for all I knew, since I had no way of catching him out. But Babar Ali had been born and brought up in his forest; both his father and uncle had been mahouts too. His life revolved around elephants, and his survival, around the forest. He had no need to bluff. It was I who didn't have the capacity to plumb the depths of his knowledge.

The elephant ambled along the forest path, snapping and tearing off small branches and leaves and munching them as it swayed from side to side. This wasn't anything like an elephant ride at the zoo. The jungle became thicker and then, suddenly, thinner. It was no longer a forest, but a watery wilderness, or a wild waterway. I had never seen such tall grass in my life. Only Mansingh's shoulders and head rose above it, the rest being covered by abnormally tall and monstrous vines. I have never seen the American prairies, but they must be something like this. This was grass only by name. The very name of such fields of grass had changed in France because soldiers used to hide in them during the Resistance. I've travelled through acres of open fields in the Camargue area of France. Those are swamps too, but the grass there cannot be compared to the grass here. There, too, wild white horses gallop away, their manes flying, raising droplets of water with their hooves, but the wild deer running here are an altogether different sight.

There the sun can split your scalp, start fires, and blaze like a desert. Here there was thunder and a darkened sky. The first drops of rain had appeared. There we had travelled in an open jeep on a man-made road. Here there was no road to speak of, the wild beasts having created their own trails with their paws. Mansingh must have been travelling along his familiar elephant route, but we could see no sign of an actual path either in front of or behind us.

'It's going to rain. You have no umbrellas. You won't be able to see anything either, Didimoni. You'll get soaked in the bargain.' Babar Ali said, 'Better to cut short the elephant trip and go back, the animals won't come out today.'

'What do you mean they won't come out? I don't see any caves or anything. Where will they hide?'

'I mean you won't be able to see too far in the rain. Not many of the animals will go out for a drink of water when it's pouring. The birds won't be flying about, the monkey won't be jumping from tree to tree.'

'Let them not. We're not going back. We're supposed to be in the jungle for three hours. We'll stay the entire time.'

'Even if you get drenched?'

'What can we do if it rains? We'll get drenched, yes.'

'Then take my umbrella at least, I don't need one.'

But the intensity of the rain made a mockery of both the umbrella and the elephant fella.

~

Dark Shadows in the Forest

Wet and bedraggled, we got off the elephant's back to look for our boat. The river waters had risen already. Incredible! Our mahout's shouts brought the boat and the boatman to us from the other bank. The rain had probably kept them away from our side of the river. The forest officer was a rather nice man. He was very relieved to see us back, for he had been quite perturbed—first, this torrential downpour, and then he had never imagined that these two women would insist on riding through the jungle on elephant back despite the rain (even if they were dressed in shirts and trousers). Drenched to the bone, we were feeling very cold now, since it was the end of October, and a chilly wind had sprung up, piercing us all the way to the memories of a previous life. Our need for a warm sanctuary drove us into the forest office. How were we to get home now? Kamrup Complex was at least a mile away, and there was no question of walking through this marauding rain. If only we could get a cup of tea and a set of dry clothes, or at least a towel. All kinds of needs and wants darted through my mind. (All this while there wasn't even a roof over our heads. Now that we had one, I needed towels, clothes, tea!)

'How did you manage this elephant ride through this driving rain....' Even the other employees were thunderstruck. 'We had expected you back much earlier. Really....'

'Come back? The stronger the rain got, the more delirious Dr Sen was with joy. The animals were hiding from the rain, so she was adamant that we find them,' explained Arghyaa. 'She did get to see them eventually. Three rhinos, two elephants, lots of deer, flocks of birds, and ...'

'And a fresh tiger pug mark,' I couldn't help adding. 'I've never been so close to a free tiger before. Following the pug marks through the tall grass....'

'Oh my god! But that's exactly where ...'

'The tigers hide? That's why we went. All the way to the river. Then we couldn't find the marks anymore, they disappeared.'

'Thank heavens,' said the forest officer. 'Why should the tiger get drenched to fulfil your desire for a view? It must have taken shelter too.'

I have observed from childhood that the one up there has some kind of equipment to hear what my heart wants, be it small or big. How else could dry towels have arrived without even asking for them? Followed by steaming cups of tea. The towels helped dry our bodies, and the tea, the dampness in our hearts. Every room in the forest bungalow was occupied. A young Punjabi couple was visiting with their parents, their baby daughter, her nanny, and their driver. We chatted for some time with them. They were having a cup of tea in the veranda, gazing at the rain. Suddenly I saw a private car setting off. I jumped up at once. 'Which way, Moshai, which way are you going? *Jaayen toh jaayen kahan?*'

'Not that one, not that one, that's not an official car,' the forest officer bellowed. 'My car will drop you as soon as it's back. This one's a private car.' Private or official, what difference did it make to me? I wasn't an officer, was I?

'Oh, this one's good enough. Caste no bar. I'm also a private citizen. Driver Moshai, oh Driver Moshai! Will you give us a lift please?' The helpless driver looked questioningly at the Punjabi gentleman. What could the gentleman possibly do? 'Of course, of course.' Any other reply would have robbed him of his status as a gentleman. Offering many thanks, waving our limbs to the accompaniment of numerous smiles, the two of us went back in the car. It was still raining. Driving into Kamrup Complex was quite difficult, since several gates had to be unlatched. The gatekeepers refused to come out in the rain. So we got out ourselves, slid beneath the gates to enter, and waved goodbye to the driver. By the time we arrived in the presence of the Phukans, laughing and jumping up and down, drenched once again, they were wan with anxiety. But Arghyaa was bubbling. The jungle was right next door, but, apparently, she had never had as much fun in it. I certainly had not. I was weak-kneed with sheer delight.

Not even the sight of three rhinos had excited me as much as the glimpse of the tiger's claws. Both the elephants were standing quietly in the rain like sages, as though they were taking a shower in the bathroom. It was the same with rhinos, though they did stir themselves on seeing us and disappeared in a flash like people running home in the rain. But the elephants did not budge, such was their confidence. So many winding trails, lakes (or ponds?), fields of grass (or of reeds?), jungle streams (or canals?), and just the one spot with a dark green covering—a dense growth of tall trees and creepers, where you had to ride on an elephant. The rest was open ground. Acres of swampland filled with tall grass. A herd of deer was running through the water in the rain. Their streaking figures, visible through gaps in the blades of grass, were as graceful as ocean waves, while the impact of their hooves raised tall fountains of white water all in a row, mingling with the rain—an unforgettable sight. With its disproportionately fat body, the horned rhinoceros in its armour of hide looks like a retired medieval warrior with a marked similarity to a painted clown. Who'd have guessed that even a creature as ponderous as the rhino could disappear in the tall grass in a flash! That too was unforgettable. I would never have experienced the irresistible grace with which animals move unless I had been to the forest. Yes, you do see a sharp animal grace in the movement of the cat or the stretching of the dog in the city, but it is concealed beneath speed, whose grace is not to be seen except in an open forest. Once, in a reserved forest in Karnataka, whose name I cannot remember (Nagarkot or Nagarcoil or something like that), I remember staring in surprise from the back of an elephant at a herd of twenty-five or thirty bison. Their astonished gaze, the music of their footsteps racing away at a moment's notice, the sudden swirl of dust raised by their galloping feet, and the flight of dry leaves, and, even before that, the way they surveyed us in silence with their white, frightened, angry eyes, still and unmoving, their horned heads lowered—all of it is embedded in my memory. I remember seeing a flash of yellow lightning too in the grass. I don't know what it was, a dog or a deer. Back at the forest office, I found a large group of people out with torches, beating on tin sheets—apparently a yellow tiger had just made off with the deer kept as a pet by the office. Obviously this was the tiger who had appeared before us like a streak of yellow lightning. Not for a moment had we imagined it could have been a tiger. Although there are tigers deep in the forest, they are never visible—that's what we had been told. Deer, nilgais, foxes, and elephants could be spotted—with luck, bison too. Clearly, luck was on my side on that occasion, as it was this time too. I even saw it raining in a forest in Assam. No small achievement. Of course, everyone said it would have been better had it not rained—there would have been many more birds in the air, more monkeys on the trees, more beasts roaming about. Never mind all that, what would I have done with more of them? The zoo had enough. Could anything but thunder, lightning, and a torrential down-pour—fat streams of water being poured from pitchers—have created such a jungle-like atmosphere? Moving about in the forest on the back of an elephant named Mansingh on a dark monsoon-like morning, amidst the rumble of black clouds and unrelenting rain ... oh! An entirely unique experience!

Arghyaa still sends me New Year greetings every year. Each time she refers to that day it rained. This tells me that the day is not just my one-of-a-kind personal treasure. There really was magic in it.

Sheela Barthakur arrived in a car with her son and husband as scheduled.

'Did you enjoy Kaziranga? The rain must have ruined everything, didn't it?'

'On the contrary. I loved it, just loved it.'

'Really?'

'I spent last night like some exotic goddess. Guarded by wild animals.'

'What do you mean?'

'I mean that the forest animals go down to the river to drink at night, right? You can hear all sorts of strange, wild sounds. The eerie whistle of night birds, the ever-present chorus of foxes and frogs, the rustling of leaves, the roars of unknown beasts in the distance, on top of which, some uninvited crea-ture seemed to have crossed the river to our side. It was rubbing itself against my cottage walls, on the side facing the river. Fortunately there are no windows or anything in that wall—but I heard the sound clearly and for a long time. I had a taste of the jungle without leaving my room. Thank you for that.'

'Yes, you do get that there. The sounds of the forest from the room. It's a frequent thing hereabouts. They were probably rhinos, they rub against things all the time. But there's nothing to be afraid of—were you frightened? Animals show up quite often to scratch themselves on our cottage walls. I should have warned you. I hope you weren't afraid or didn't try to go out or anything.'

'Of course not, are you mad? Why should I go out? Not that I'm particularly used to being in forests, but as a student in California, I remember going camping in the Yosemite National Park. At night bears were scratching themselves on the canvas of our tents, even rummaging in discarded cans for leftover food. I had almost run out of my tent in joy at spotting bears, but my girlfriend held me back. She said even if they're not dangerous, grizzly bears aren't decent people.'

'You can never trust wild animals. Who knows what they'll do?'

'This was my first night alone amidst such wonderful jungle sounds. Thank goodness the animal came, I should be grateful to it.'

'We should have asked Arghyaa to stay with you.'

'But why? I really had no problems. I wasn't afraid at all. Not one bit.'

There were plenty of books and volumes of poetry here. Jagdish Phukan was a friend of our friend Hamdi Bey's, as well as of the poet Nirendranath Chakraborty's. Requesting me to invite them on his behalf, he added that whenever I needed solitude and rest to write, the warm hospitality of Kaziranga Inn would always be available.

'Where's the money? I can't afford this.'

'Who's asking you for payment?' Jagdish scolded me. 'A wonderful piece from your pen is all the payment we need.

Hospitality is just that—hospitality. We live all by ourselves in the forest. We're very happy when we get like-minded friends here. You must come, come whenever you like. You have a standing invitation to visit your friends. Tell Niren and Hamdi too.'

This was in 1977, when the movement to oust foreigners from Assam had not yet started. Politics had not yet begun beating its blood-soaked drums to drown the murmurs of the love for art. The warm, affectionate, enlightened, unassuming, venerable face of Assam that I saw has been distorted afterwards in different ways by newspapers and the radio, letters from Assam, reports in magazines, and refugees. It is difficult to reconcile the images I had seen for myself with the subsequent ones thrown at us.

But I believe that humanism wins the endgame. This is a temporary aberration of the mind, political sleight-of-hand, the Indian rope trick. This is not our soul.

Sheela Barthakur was on her way back home after the conference, along with husband, son, and chief guest. Our car was driven onto a ferry steamer to cross the Brahmaputra. It could accommodate six cars in a row. We took seats on the first-floor deck. One could sit in a shaded veranda with a cup of tea. We were on our way to Tezpur. Sheela had said that going back from Jorhat without visiting Tezpur did not amount to visiting Assam. I hadn't even been to Guwahati—never even met the Brahmaputra. Tezpur was to the north, in a mountainous area. It was a beautiful spot, with green forests and hills, not to mention the Brahmaputra. Not flat like Jorhat. Nor colourless. Although I had quite liked Jorhat too. So very different from Calcutta, after all. Plenty of open spaces. Take Rani and her husband Bijoy Hendrique's house—so much of the grounds was overrun by wild plants. There seemed to be a pond too, and I noticed a paddy field as well. Naturally, there was a garden full of flowers. And how amazingly beautiful the house was! Rabindranath and his son Rathindranath must have learnt the artistic use of wood, bamboo, and cane in such houses in Assam and Tripura. Bijoy's father was still living at the time of my visit. What remains is his enormous library with its memories of scholarship.

~

The Great Brahmaputra

The view of the Brahmaputra from the ferry boat filled my heart. The river was so wide that the opposite bank was not visible. Green dots—islands full of forests—could be seen in the distance. My first thought was that I had never seen a river with so many islands. But no, I had. In Germany. There were numerous hilly islands on the Rhine, with ancient forts on them. I took a long boat ride on the Rhine once. The multitude of islands and the stately grace of the forts on them were stunning. They seemed out of a fairy tale. There are many rocky islands on the Ganga at Bhagalpur too. Gaibinath is one of them, but there are many others. British artists of the eighteenth and nineteenth centuries have left a number of sketches of those islands.

But I had never seen such things in Bangladesh. My eyes have travelled much, seen a great deal. But the heart seeks to wander everywhere in Bengal. By Bangladesh, I am not referring only to the country which goes by that name. My heart mourns this system of naming, for Bangladesh refers to the birthplace of Bengalis, where the Bengali language is spoken—East or West Bengal come only afterwards. To give one portion the entirety of the name Bangladesh, while the other is just West Bengal, is the kind of meaningless nomenclature, devoid of both tradition and logic—that is not to be seen anywhere else in the world. Does anyone call them

Korea and North Korea? Or Vietnam and South Vietnam? Or Germany and West Germany? Only in the case of Bengal have we created this convenient arrangement. We have both made it and accepted it. No one suffers as a result. I am no longer an inhabitant of 'Bangladesh'. Deprived of my home state without being made homeless. We used to live outside Bengal for a long time, but it was to Bangladesh that we would return from Delhi during holidays. That didn't necessarily mean Dhaka or Chittagong alone, but also Calcutta or Santiniketan.

Anyway, I had not yet had the fortune of seeing the extraordinary rivers of East Bengal. I had only read in books about sandbars, about islands rising from the river. Then I recollected our Sunderban, where too there are a great many islands formed by the deposition of silt. I remember teaching my daughter the speciality of these islands in the Brahmaputra as part of her geography course.

There was still some time for the ferry to leave. I had a bunch of white flowers in my hand, which Mrs Phukan had given me. On an impulse, I leant over the railing and tossed one of them into the Brahmaputra. It was borne far away in the twinkling of an eye. How marvellous! A river so broad that its banks were not visible, but how strong its current was! Like a little mountain torrent.

Oho, is that why they call you a male river then, a *nad*, and not a female, a *nodi*? Is it because of your invincible speed, your irresistible power? If you'd been female, you'd have been more sedate, more serene. Quieter, more civil, with a heavier gait. Like the Ganga, the Yamuna, the Narmada, or the Godavari. But then no matter how fabulous Punjab's *panchnad* are, there's no lack of male rivers here in Bengal. West Bengal alone has the Damodar, the Rupnarayan, the Ajay, the Dwarakeshwar, and the Barakar. There we are, the famous five. The names of these five class-one officers spring to mind immediately. Sometimes they are only knee-deep, displaying their ribs of sand, sprawled with their teeth bared, like skeletons. But at other times they are like a Kumbhkarna awakened suddenly, rushing forward with the blessings of open sluice gates, sweeping away people in villages. The Brahmaputra is adept at flooding too, but surely it has never had a famished and withered body of sand, with water that is barely knee- or waist-high, or not even ankle-deep at times. In East Bengal, the very name of the Arial Khan River conjures up visions of a general, anger blazing in his eyes, an unsheathed sword in hand. Similarly, the name Brahmaputra makes one think of a rider on a galloping white horse, a feather in his milk-white turban.

On a whim I kept tearing off flowers from the bunch in my hand and tossing them into the currents, *Om Brahmaputray Mahanaday Namah*. The river caught each one of them at once, relaying them in an instant to the distant island in the middle. Flower Number One may well have dropped anchor in the rock-strewn mud of the island by now. I had become quite friendly with the Brahmaputra already. It might be noble in appearance, but its behaviour is certainly not as regal as a VIP's should be. Just like the formidable tiger Khairi would play with a tiny rubber ball, the gigantic Brahmaputra also seemed to be playing a flower game with me.

~

Jeep-babu

A Bengali gentleman was also travelling on the ferry in his jeep. The vehicle had yellow printed curtains—I was charmed instantly. Then I spotted tender young faces through gaps in the curtain. His wife and children were all in there, all of them speaking in Bengali. 'Where are you from?'

'Tezpur.'

'Are you going to Tezpur?'

'We are. He's going to Bomdila.'

'Bomdila? I've been trying to find out where Bomdila is. How far is it from Tezpur?'

'Not too far.'

'Didn't the Chinese come as far as Bomdila?'

'Thank goodness they didn't make it to Tezpur,' Sheela said. 'There was great fear in Tezpur, though, that the Chinese are coming. Many people abandoned their homes.'

'But the Chinese went back from Bomdila—along the Lhasa–Tawang Road.'

'They constructed a fantastic road in just ten days, you know,' said Jeep-babu. 'It's still an excellent road; I believe there's been no damage.'

'Tawang? Is that where the Tawang Monastery is? Isn't there a direct road from Bomdila?'

'Yes, the Chinese entered India through Tawang. That's where the border with Tibet is, the McMahon Line.'

~

For the Sheer Joy of It

'Can you tell me how to get to Tawang?'

'What's that? Tawang? Why Tawang all of a sudden? Do you work on Tibetan history? That's true, you'll get plenty of material there....'

'...'

'No? You have no interest in Tibetan history? Why Tawang then? I see, you must be specializing in philosophy. Yes, for Buddhist philosophy ...'

'...'

'Not that either? Neither history nor philosophy? Then what? Wait, I know, Sino-Tibetan languages, right? No?'

Now the gentleman looked genuinely perturbed. 'Is it anthropology, then? The *Mompa* versus *Khampa* conflict? Tribal culture? Not those either? Ah, now I get it. Political science. Border dispute, McMahon Line. Isn't that it? Have I got it or not? Chinese aggression, Lhasa–Tawang Road. Bomdila occupation. Four dates of the twentieth century are important for you—1914, 1937–8–9, 1951, and 1962. Yes, Sir, Tawang is quite important positionally!'

'But I'm not researching any of this. I'm not even remotely interested in researching Tawang. I just want very much to go there. In 1975, I heard from a philosopher-friend of mine in Shillong [Rita Gupta] that there are many rare Tibetan manuscripts there. But it's a very difficult journey. Not too many people make it that far, I'm told. Verrier Elwin did visit a few years ago, though.'

'So did Kamala Devi Chattopadhyay, but she couldn't go back.'

'What do you mean? Isn't she in Delhi now?'

'Maybe she is now, but she wasn't for a long time. She was marooned in Tawang. The road was cut off by snow. She would have spent the entire winter there had it not been for someone having a heart attack.'

'What! Who had a heart attack? Was it a relative?'

'No, it wasn't anyone she knew. An army officer posted in Tawang. He was airlifted to Bomdila in a military helicopter— and, along with him, Kamala Devi Chattopadhyay. An elderly lady, what if something were to happen to her in that extreme cold? That's the only reason—or else military vehicles are not allowed to give rides to civilian women.'

'Were you in Tawang too?'

'Of course not, why should I kill myself in the cold, that too in a place nobody goes to? You know it's above the tree line, don't you? There are no large trees, no birds and animals. It's a lousy place. No one visits out of choice. Nothing to see, except Tibetan yaks and Buddhist monks. That's what you want to see, right? Useless stuff! The monastery is India's biggest though. The second largest in the world. The biggest one is in Lhasa. People talk of the one in Dharamshala or the one in Leh, but they're much smaller. There's no larger library anywhere. More than two thousand books and manuscripts. To put it simply? A manuscript library, right? Even includes books written in letters of gold. But they won't let you touch those. Every one of them is wrapped in a fabric of bark, tied with string, and put away safely. I believe they're dusted and cleaned regularly, though. But no one can read them. How many people can read ancient Tibetan, after all? What do you want to go for? Do you know how to read ancient Tibetan?'

'I can't, I can't. I keep telling you it's not for research. Pure curiosity. So that I can say, "I climbed the mountain because it's there". Tawang's there, so I want to go.'

'Why not go to Guwahati instead? Guwahati's there too. Much easier and safer to travel there, and plenty to see. Have you been to Kamakhyadevi? Gauhati University? Cotton College?'

'No. I will, one day. But Tawang first. How do you know so much about Tawang if you've never been there yourself?'

'I've been in Bomdila a long time, haven't I? We get all the news at Bomdila. Army people come down from the Tawang area all the time. Of course, Tawang itself is a military-free area, neither Indian nor Chinese army camps are allowed within forty miles on either side of the border.'

'What a good arrangement! No border guards then?'

'There are. But they are stationed on the border. Apparently the Indian and Chinese soldiers eat and drink together. Our last military camp this side of the border is at a place named Jung. An open camp, that is. I'm positive we have secret bunkers and an underground campus in Tawang. Nothing will be visible on the surface. All subterranean.'

'Really? I'm getting goosebumps. This is like one of the Ghana-da stories. Now I'm even more excited. I'll see the subterranean bunkers, lovely. Never seen one before.'

'You think they'll let you in? My foot! Are you expecting them to invite you cordially to see the bunkers? Those things are top secret. Even the residents of Tawang have never been told about them. I have no idea what you're thinking. It's a very sensitive area, you know. Have you got an inner line permit? It's all very well to jump up and down saying you want to go there, but can you get hold of a permit? Do you know anyone?'

'An inner line permit? What on earth is that? Where do you get it?'

'It's the government's permission for entering this reserved area. A passport, basically. Issued by the Arunachal government. They don't give it to anyone and everyone. You have to provide a reason. A valid reason.'

'Where must I go to get one?'

'Itanagar. You have to go to Itanagar.'

'Which way is Itanagar? How far from Tezpur? Is it on the way to Bomdila?'

'It's in the opposite direction.'

'Really? This is going to be a problem. And you're going off to Bomdila the day after tomorrow.'

'What's that got to do with you?'

'I was thinking of going up to Bomdila in your jeep.'

'You can come along if you get the permit. I don't have any particular objection. But where will you stay at Bomdila? I can't let you stay at my place. My family isn't there right now. Arrangements will have to be made at the Inspection Bungalow. But what'll you go to Bomdila for anyway? There's nothing to see there. And Tawang is a long way off from Bomdila, you know. Besides, who are you going to Tawang with? Get hold of a companion first. You never know what might happen in those places, you mustn't go alone.'

~

Who Wants to Cross Over?

'A companion? How on earth will I find a companion? All right, wait, let me ask Sheela. She's quite enthusiastic, who knows, she might agree.'

Sheela was astonished at first. Then she became very worried, and finally a little annoyed too, I suspected. What kind of madness was this on the part of her chief guest, that too in the presence of her husband and son? How could a women's literary conference maintain its status this way? What must her husband and son have thought? Surely they'd be laughing silently. They would definitely joke about this afterwards. So she tried to persuade me not to go. 'Why Tawang at this time of the year? It's a very difficult road, and so cold besides. You seem to have brought only this one blanket. I have many things to attend to at home, so much work piled up because I'd been preoccupied with the literary conference. I have to supervise my son's studies. It's not convenient for me to travel now. And who'll go with you? Moreover, you need an overcoat, muffler, monkey cap, gloves, woollen socks, shoes, thick sweaters, thermal underwear, and lots more. Do you plan to buy all this now? Very expensive. You must have these clothes at home already, considering you've lived abroad for so long. I know, of course, that writers and poets are a little eccentric, but this is too much. You don't really need to go to Tawang urgently. Why not just spend ten days with us here in Tezpur? You could visit Dibrugarh or Duliajan instead. You have a standing invitation from Niti already. You'll see how lavishly they do things at Oil India. They'll keep you in the lap of luxury. They'll look after you every moment. Besides, you're not well. I can see how often you have to take medicines. Who gave you this idea of going to Tawang? Give up the thought.'

Here she was, taking me to Tezpur with such solicitousness that I couldn't possibly quarrel with her. But I am prone to wanderlust. Once the idea of travelling somewhere occurs to me, I give it everything I've got. If it still doesn't material-ize, so be it. But I had no intention of giving up just because someone was telling me to. I consoled Sheela, 'Not at all, you don't have to go with me. But do you have an overcoat? And thick sweaters? A monkey cap?'

A surprised Sheela said, 'An overcoat? I do. No monkey cap.'

'Will you lend me the coat? You'll definitely get it back if I'm alive.'

'What a terrible thing to say. Why shouldn't I get it back? Of course, I'll lend you my coat. But I wish you weren't going.'

'I believe I have to go to Itanagar to get an inner line per-mit. Have you any idea how to get there?'

'There's no need to go to Itanagar.' Sheela's husband finally spoke up. 'It's available right here in Tezpur, at the office of the Arunachal ADC. I know them, I'll get you one.' This was manna from heaven. It was just that he was married to some-one else, for I was inspired to embrace Mr Barthakur. I hadn't exchanged a single word with either him or his son all this time. Neither of them was particularly chatty. But I had observed Mr Barthakur helping his wife tirelessly during the confer-ence. The teenaged son had slaved away too, serving food and making endless trips in the car to help the guests get to their destinations. Sheela really was very fortunate. Homemakers do not usually get the cooperation of their husband or children when it comes to activities beyond the household. They get taunts instead. But Sheela Barthakur had pulled it off with the help of her family. Not that I saw too many male volunteers, though. The women did all the hard work.

'It would be better to abandon the plan to visit Tawang,' said Mr Barthakur, 'but if you do need the inner line permit, I'll get them to give you one.'

'What will you do with the coat if you don't have a companion?' asked Jeep-babu. 'There's no question of travelling alone. How will you get to Tawang anyway? Where will you stay? You'll have to make all your arrangements right here in Tezpur. There's no point rushing to Bomdila with me. You can always take the local bus from Tezpur to Bomdila. Make all the arrangements first—clear, complete, definite arrangements. Don't leave before you do. What's the use of going to Bomdila right away? You'll just be stranded.'

I hate unsolicited advice. I'll do as I please. So long as I don't go in your jeep, right? So long as I don't stay at your house. I assure you I shan't. I'll do it my way. I'm damned if I'm going to hang on to your coat-tails. While muttering all these imprecations in my head, what I actually said was, 'Never mind, no need to worry about me. I'll work something out. I'll go if things fall into place, and if they don't, I won't. No need to worry your heads off. There, we've arrived at the jetty.' The boat was indeed being moored. 'There's Tezpur!' The cry rose from the deck.

'Here's my phone number in Tezpur. I'm leaving at one-thirty in the afternoon the day after tomorrow. Let me know if you can make all the arrangements tomorrow.' Scribbling his number on a scrap of paper, the gentleman handed it to me. He couldn't have been as bad a person as I had thought. He was certainly well-informed about Tawang. I'd learnt a great deal from his admonitions, and my enthusiasm had risen. I put the phone number away safely.

~

A Heart Filled with Light

We had arrived at Tezpur. Disembarking, we walked across a stretch of sand to reach the riverbank. Sheela said, 'We'll take you to the house where you'll be staying. They have a phone. Bengalis, but they've been living here for three or four generations. They're particularly fond of your books. They'll be very angry with me if you don't stay with them, which is why I'm taking you there. You won't misunderstand, will you? I'll be delighted if you move to my place in a day or two. I'll have got the house organized by then. We've been away a long time, so everything is in a mess. It would have been troublesome for you right now.'

Oh lord. Me and troublesome! But how was Sheela Barthakur to know that disorganized households no longer troubled me in the least. It was she who would have been troubled. She was not mentally prepared to look after a guest, for the poor thing had had to take care of numerous people all these days.

~

The Book of Preparation

'Here's Dr Dev Sen. We're not stopping though. This is our Mrs Bose, this is Professor Bose.'

'*Nomoshkar*.'

'Welcome, welcome. Just finished your Kumbh Mela. Fantastic. But your essays are also ...'

(Grateful, embarrassed sounds.)

'How did your literary conference at Jorhat go?' This was for Sheela.

'It was wonderful. But back-breaking.'

'Come in. You can't leave at once, Mr Barthakur, you must have a cup of coffee or tea. You must be exhausted after such a long journey....'

'Not now, there's so much to do at home. Another time, thank you, thank you.' The Barthakurs left.

Within minutes Professor Bose and Mrs Bose had been converted to Dada and Alo-di. A schoolboy appeared a little later, as tall as Calcutta's Shahid Minar, with a head of curly hair—he was also the junior table-tennis champion of Assam. Shami began to address me as Mashi in the blink of an eye. I found a permanent place almost instantaneously in Alo-di's shiny bright household, almost as perfect and proud as the ones run by German homemakers. As I sprawled on Alo-di's bed chatting with her, or running my fingers through Shami's hair while he lay on his back with a Tintin comic near his nose, I felt as though I had been in Tezpur a year already.

The trouble began when it came to Tawang. Dada was much older, and prone to anxiety. Also to protectiveness. He was foremost among the crème de la crème of Tezpur. I couldn't very well dismiss his viewpoint while living in his own house. A man as eminent as Professor Bose was not at all keen on my going to Tawang. Alo-di wasn't in favour of taking such risks either. Only Shami was supportive. He wouldn't be able to come along though; his exams were approaching. But he continued to provide moral courage.

'Why aren't you letting Mashi go? Do you think she's like the two of you? She tried to climb the Matterhorn. I read in *Anandamela*. [She couldn't scale the peak though, she ended up in a chicken coop instead.] Would you have allowed her to go to the Kumbh? I'm sure you wouldn't have. And no one would have got to read the story. Considering you yourselves keep saying what a wonderful piece it is (I haven't read it yet though)....'

When even this didn't work: 'Do you think you two are Mashi's guardians? She's an adult. She can be a chief guest at a festival, but she can't go to Tawang? You're not treating her like a grown-up, just like you don't allow me to drive. You'd better stay with the Barthakurs, Mashi. You can go to Tawang from their house. You don't know these people, they're very difficult. They'll be so protective of you, they'll turn your life into a living hell.'

Now Alo-di protested vehemently.

'Have I told you not to go? All I said was that it's extremely risky. It's only your father who's protesting.'

Which he indeed was.

'You can be the most accomplished and knowledgeable person in the world,' he said, 'but all by yourself, amongst hill tribals and the military ... no, it's not advisable. No one's invited you to be the chief guest there, have they? A woman, after all. And a dangerous age, at that. No one from your family on either side is here—we're like your family now. No, you're being far too impulsive. It's not the same as going to the Kumbh Mela. Everyone's a pilgrim there. One objective, clean hearts. People stick together automatically over there. But no one's accompanying you here. Not just that, no one ever goes there. It's neither a pilgrim spot nor a tourist resort. A god-forsaken place, a reserved area, only army people and tribals and Buddhist lamas live there. And extremely unpredictable too. For one thing, hill people never bathe. Nor are they used to tourists. We don't even know their customs. Who knows when you might offend someone, and then they'll behead you at once. You might trespass on army territory and they might shoot you dead. I don't think such risks ...'

Alo-di interrupted him suddenly.

'Cutting her head off or shooting her dead will all come later. First, she has to get there. How will she? No trains, no flights, no cars, nothing. Wishes aren't horses. How will you get there? Impossible. You can't go.'

I protested vehemently.

'There's a bus to Bomdila every day. I'll find a way from there. But the first thing is the permit. Where's the office of the Arunachal ADC?'

'I know where it is.' Shami leapt to his feet.

'So do I,' grumbled Dada.

'Isn't it next to whatsit?' said Alo-di.

'Since all of you know, shall we go?'

'It's not that simple. How will we get a driver at this hour? Besides, the office has closed. It's long past five.'

An exquisitely beautiful lady appeared suddenly.

'I came to meet you,' she said. Alo-di introduced us. 'Dr Prabodh Chandra Sen's daughter. Get the connection? He's from your Santiniketan. Our Ila-di.'

Ila-di really was a lovely person. She wasn't in the least bit astonished when I asked within two minutes, 'Do you have a monkey cap?'

'A monkey cap? I don't, but my father-in-law has one. Why, though?'

'Why indeed. Don't ask.' Alo-di proceeded to explain things to Ila-di. 'Utter madness. Says I want to go to Tawang. See the monastery. No prior arrangements, no clothes, no permit, no one she knows there. That's what the monkey cap is for. Don't give it to her, I'm warning you.'

'If you don't give it to me I'll go in a shawl. What about gloves?'

'My father-in-law has those too. He's very old, can't stand the cold. Uses woollen gloves.'

'Perfect, that will do. Now for sweaters.'

'You can use my sweaters, Mashi, I have plenty. Ma knits me new ones every year.' Shami was prepared.

'Baba's sleeveless sweater, my pullover, Sheela Barthakur's coat,' he counted, 'Ila-Mashi's father-in-law's cap and gloves....'

'And socks and shoes? You'd better give her yours, Shami,' said Alo-di.

'Mine?' Pulling out a shoe eighteen inches in length, Shami raised his eyebrows as high as they would go. 'My shoes? Are you cra ... zy? You could take my socks though. They'll keep you warm up to your knees. You'll have to buy shoes. Don't you have shoes, Ma? Only slippers and sandals? *Tchah!*'

'She'll need snow boots. Why don't you give her the boots you play in?' Alo-di piped up again.

'I would have. If only they had fitted her. But look at her feet, as small as yours. Tchah! You call these a sportsman's feet? You could buy a good pair of keds, Mashi. North Star.'

'Grand idea. It'll be easiest to climb in keds. I'll buy a pair. Two pairs of socks will be enough to keep my feet warm, won't they?' I was feeling confident now.

'You're really going?' Ila-di was startled. 'I thought it was all a joke.'

It was natural that no woman would believe that the lady chief guest of the Assam Women's Literature Conference was seriously planning to visit Tawang in borrowed clothes. She had to be insane. No one except the sixteen-year-old Shami could see that my plan was a concrete one. It was obvious to me that the impression I had gathered of adults in my childhood was accurate. My theory is that the brain is uncluttered in childhood. As children we are used to seeing things exactly as they are, the pure truth. The older we get, the more confused we become. Constant exposure to contaminated reality and corrupted truth clouds our vision, so that the unreal and the untrue seem real and true. The face of simple truth becomes so unfamiliar that it appears either tragically vanquished, or a distant reality, incorporeal and imaginary. Or else, extremely complex and dangerous. Some people overcome this weakness over a period of time, and come to be known as saints and sages. Civilized, cultured people misread things at first. Sometimes, on second thoughts and detailed consideration, they correct themselves. But the immediate response of the young is the right one. What Shami could see easily because of his youth was not visible to any of the others because they had grown up. A week-long trip, not exactly a desolate spot devoid of human contact, with the presence of the military implying law and order. There may not have been any Bengali or Assamese people there, but that didn't mean there was no one at all. How ridiculous was it not to consider anyone but middle-class babus human? Whether it was tribals or the army or Buddhist lamas, they had excellent social systems—well-organized and disciplined. Why did I have to be afraid of them? Anything beyond middle-class society means unknown territory, outside the Lakshman Rekha. To set foot there is to invite troubles and dangers of all sorts. You're dead the moment you step beyond the ramparts of soft sand created by middle-class values and philosophy. The end of the world!

Visiting the Kumbh Mela does not amount to transgressing middle-class principles, even if you travel all alone. But Tawang?

What does this mean?

Why must you go? Why do you have to go?

Who will benefit from such a trip? Not on business, not on a pilgrimage, not to boost your health, not for a job, not on academic research. Why, then?

To collect material for your books?

Not that either. Just to prove that that wasn't the reason, I deliberately didn't write the story of Tawang for five years.

Why, then?

What do you mean why? Pure madness.

Mere whimsy.

It's not good for women to be whimsical.

It's not good for women to be obstinate.

It's not good for women to be so bold.

Of course, if it were a man now....

A man has the right. He can kick middle-class values in the face and choose a different life. Men see nothing threatening or objectionable in this. Such personal revolts have always existed. It hasn't destroyed human society. There are always a few eccentrics in the world.

But women?

Shame! Eccentricity is not for women.

Oh my god, what do you mean! How will the world ever survive? The woman is the goddess of the household, its Lakshmi. She is the one to preserve its peace and grace. The most threatening thing for a peaceful family of man and woman is the wife's mind taking unscheduled flights into the horizon.

Do you think anyone loves a woman of boundless spirit?

No one does.

You think anyone sympathizes with her?

No one does.

You think anyone washes her soiled clothes? Or serves her dinner on a gleaming plate and fans her while she eats?

No one does, no one does. No one can be bothered to ease the way for wayward women.

In every storybook I've read, the more shamelessly profligate a man is, the more women love him. They fuss over him, take care of his needs, wash his underwear, starch and iron his clothes. They fall head over heels in love with him. From Sarat Chandra Chatterjee and Premankur Atarthi and Prabodh Sanyal in our mothers' times to Kalkut and Buddhadev Guha in ours, it's the same experience everywhere. As for poor Nillohit, he keeps falling in love. It's not as though absolutely no one falls in love with him, though—as a matter of fact, a few young women have fallen in love with him too. But not as often as in the case of Kalkut or Prabodh Sanyal. For they themselves are not the 'lover' type; they are detached, they are philosophers, they love the entire world. They are like Tarapada in Rabindranath's story *Atithi* or like the currents of the Ganga. 'You have nothing to hold you back and so you are a free spirit.' But when it comes to me, neither of these two materializes. I don't fall in love with anyone, nor does anyone fall in love with me. Yes, I can hear you say, at this age, with your daughters growing up, what a thing to talk about! Quite. What about Dev Anand, isn't he getting old? Is Kishore Kumar's son a baby? Am I the only one getting on in years? I travel so much, I travel all the time, from one country to another, from conferences to pilgrimages. Could there not have been a potential lover in even one of these places? Of course, there could have. But it's because of the flaws in my nature that there aren't any. Now the thing is, which is more important? To live in complete freedom or to be in love and under someone's rule? There's too much trouble involved in being in love; hope and disappointment, meetings and separations, hurt and despair in no small measure. And besides, lovers are terribly possessive creatures. Just like policemen. They'll imprison you in love. And freedom is forbidden. That's why I always discourage love indirectly. Encouraging love means going into custody. Of course, what if I could encourage a one-way version and then vanish blithely with a smiling face like the Kalkuts of the world? That would be a different story altogether. But I'm not clever enough for that. Eventually I'll get entangled and fall head over heels in love—you never know, I might even get married, settle down in the kitchen, and start running a household. That's why I fall in love in a winner-takes-all way, at a superhuman level. Sometimes with the Ganga, sometimes with the Himalayas. With the Brahmaputra or with Tibet. Just consider the hundred per cent opportunities I get to fall in love. No relatives or family elders nearby, no friends to keep an eye on me, not even inquisitive neighbours. I travel to places where isolation follows me around like a shadow. Where solitude is available readily. Where there is no hurt or anguish, where I have to bear no responsibilities.

I may not look it, but I *am* a bit of an old-fashioned romantic. It would be impossible not to be. So are Sanskrit teachers with shaven heads and the traditional tuft of hair! Grumpy maths teachers too.

And, let me tell you a secret, there is indeed someone who maintains a constant vigil to protect daredevil women travellers, supplying caution to the imprudent, smoothening the path for those like me who welcome an uncharted course in life. There's just the one entity in the whole world who can do this, but this one entity is as good as a hundred men.

And since this personage doesn't write novels, this important fact remains unknown. Therefore, there are no wayward heroines in Bengali literature. Is there even a single woman with wanderlust? Someone who wanders around but isn't a minstrel. Not a sage, but still restless. A working woman from a middle-class family, but within whose restive heart a different sensibility is at work. Someone who is driven by a nomadic spirit to the edge of the forest.

Yet we see such men in books all the time. Their capricious ways are their main attraction. Their reckless nature is the trademark of their effervescent and eternal youth. Because men love being wayward themselves, they don't like women following suit. Leave alone offering sustenance, no one will arrange even a place to sit for the wayward heroine—neither the male reader nor the female. Novels with such heroines will never sell. Therefore, let others wander around like wayward women to collect material for their books. I shall not.

'Then why go?' It all stops at that original question. From Jeep-babu to Alo-di, from the Barthakurs to Ila-di, everyone has the same question. The same astonishment. A very valid question in a civilized world.

'Any valid reason?'

It's difficult enough to find reasons for half the work I do that will be considered valid by a civilized society. Now I was in even more trouble.

Why must everything have a reason, for heaven's sake? Why is an explanation necessary?

Since I am not an explorer, not a participant in the Kon-Tiki expedition or the conquest of Mount Everest, neither a Heyerdahl nor a Hillary, must I be tied down with a 'reason'?

I wasn't trying to discover new places. I wasn't going to break or create a record. Nor to be useful to anyone. I was going only on an impulse, entirely my own, just out of the natural curiosity that life brings, the delight of living. Was this not a valid enough reason?

I've noticed that people all over the world consider me their 'ward' very quickly. I never lack for guardians willing to take my responsibility. Is this a special technique used by the one who eases my way? A sport controlled from behind the scenes? He creates impediments, but also provides allies.

'This girl won't listen,' Alo-di told Dada finally. 'She's a Kumbh veteran.'

'You really will go? Then we must try to get the inner line permit in the morning. We'll get there in the first hour. What do you think, Alo? But whom will she go with? How will she get there?'

'By jeep. Here, a gentleman with this phone number is going up to Bomdila tomorrow. A Bengali. His wife and children live in Tezpur.'

'Where did you get hold of this one?'

'On that ferry boat.'

'What does he do in Bomdila?'

'I have no idea.'

'You didn't ask him what he did there?'

'No, should I have asked?'

'Brilliant. An unidentified man. Only a phone number. What's his name?'

'I didn't ask that either.'

'Splendid! And you've made up your mind to travel with him?'

'More or less. What'll I do with a name?'

'Where will you stay?'

'I'll have to try for the Inspection Bungalow.'

'You have to book it in advance.'

'I could also try once I get there. I'm alone, no fuss. I'm sure something will be worked out.'

'The fuss is *because* you're alone. What do you mean something will be worked out? What if it isn't? Has the man offered to put you up too?'

'No, he has said he won't let me stay at his house. His family isn't with him there. Else he would have.'

'Just as well. Perhaps he is a decent chap after all. Let me find out who he is. Give me the number.'

Dada left with the phone number.

He was back a little later, having found out every last thing over the phone. The gentleman is just that—a gentleman. A businessman in Bomdila.

'He's from Tezpur. Nothing to worry about. It's all right. You can go. But not to Tawang or anything. Up to Bomdila. Go and see how far the Chinese came, then return on the bus. Ring us. We'll pick you up at the bus stop.'

That night Dada took us for a drive around Tezpur. A lake filled with lotus blooms, green parks next to small temples hewn out of hillsides—such a beautiful town, really. He showed me a new monastery and temple. Jeep-babu lived nearby. We passed his house too. The jeep with the yellow curtains was parked in the portico. I was delighted to spot it. Ah! I'd be in that jeep on the road to Bomdila tomorrow. We even got a glimpse of the Brahmaputra by night.

This ancestral house of Professor Bose's was next to the market, half of which apparently used to be owned by his grandfather. They were a family of lawyers. Professor Bose too had a law degree, though he did not practice law.

Even in places like Allahabad or Bhagalpur or Cuttack, I've observed that the majority of Bengali settlers are either lawyers or doctors. At one time, Bengali professionals used to travel to other towns across the country in search of work, instead of joining the cutthroat competition in Calcutta.

And now? Even if there are opportunities elsewhere, there's no security.

~

The Inner Line

The trouble began next morning, at the office which issued inner line permits. It was an endless wait outside, with no one calling us in. Eventually Professor Bose forced his way into one of the rooms to find out, and they sent us to another room, where they had chairs for visitors. That was the only improvement in our status. We continued to sit, without my name being called, because we had been warned not to enter unless called. We weren't allowed to rush in shamelessly like starving people. Strict rules. As we sat there we learnt that the ADC was in Itanagar. He was the only one who could issue an inner line permit. The information came from a bearer. There was a chamber directly opposite. On an impulse I walked in through the swing doors to discover a man occupying an enormous chair. Professor Bose came with me too, and struck up an acquaintance with the man. He confirmed the same thing. Professor Bose said, 'Could you please find out about a permit over the phone?' The man sent for someone and passed on the request. He went into another room to make the phone call. We waited. I asked the man about the different ways to get to Tawang. He said there was a weekly bus service, but that this week's bus had left yesterday. The next trip would be seven days later.

'Besides the bus? No other way?'

'There is. Jeeps arrive here from Tawang quite often. Medical services jeeps, engineering services jeeps. An engineer was here; he was supposed to have left this afternoon, but his jeep needs repairs. He will go tomorrow.'

'Go where? To Tawang?'

'Yes, that's where he's posted.'

'I want to go, I want to go. Not this jeep, I'll take that jeep then. Direct to Tawang!'

'That depends on Mr Engineer. It's up to him.'

'Can't you put in a word for me? I'm sure he'll agree if you do.'

'If I can meet him.'

'Where is he staying? Is there a phone? Can I tell him myself?'

'Here at our guest house. But he's not there now, he's getting his jeep repaired.'

The man we were talking to was not a Bengali. He spoke in Hindi and was incredibly civil, but he didn't seem very keen on helping me.

~

Enter the Dragon

'Can you tell me the fate of the engineer's jeep?'

A young man entered through the swing doors with these words, his legs twice or even three times as long as his torso. He seemed to be walking on stilts. Like a model for Gwalior or Raymond's suiting, his appearance was dominated by his trousers, with the portion clad in a shirt being abbreviated, and the head with the thick-framed glasses even more so. Freshly bathed. He had Brylcreem in his hair, and flecks of talcum powder were visible on the hair on his chest, above the unbuttoned expanse of his shirt. His enormous shoes squeaked noisily as he walked in. Not just that, they were well-polished too.

Traditionally, the young men in such visions are considered heroes. Matinee-idol looks, meaning 'tall, dark, and handsome'. Quite a handsome young man, bluish eyes and all; but on seeing us he just wilted before he could finish what he was saying. He had been speaking as he entered, and was not expecting to see us. Possibly no one ever visited this office. It wasn't clear whether he was surprised or embarrassed, or what the source of his discomfort was. But he did not speak anymore.

'Just what we were talking about,' the officer told him. 'It hasn't been repaired yet. The engineer is still over there.'

'At the workshop?'

'Exactly.'

'But what if it isn't repaired today? I simply have to leave tomorrow. I have urgent work at the hospital.'

'A ration truck is leaving tomorrow. If the jeep isn't available you can hitch a lift in the truck. Since it's urgent.'

'In that case can you arrange for it?'

'Yes, I'll inform them.'

Now! Unless I asked at this moment there wouldn't be another opportunity.

I needed to ask before Gwalior Suiting exited through the swing doors.

'Excuse me, are you going to Tawang?'

He proceeded to leave the room without a glance at me. Without answering. But I was indomitable.

'Oh Moshai! You! The tall gentleman! I'm asking you.'

'You're talking to me?'

The tall man jumped as though he'd seen a ghost and turned to look in our direction. Just one look.

'Yes, of course I'm talking to you. Are you going to Tawang?'

'Yes, my jeep's broken down. So I was looking for a lift in the engineer's jeep. But that one's broken down too. Extraordinary, I tell you!'

He answered with his eyes on Professor Bose, refusing to address me, refusing even to glance at me.

'It's a tough road, you see, so cars break down frequently. They need servicing constantly.' The officer explained.

'So it seems all the jeeps are out of commission. What is this ration truck thing? The one you're planning to take. Does it take other passengers? Will it take me?'

'You?' Finally he looked directly at me.

'You're going to Tawang? Not in a truck. You can't go in a truck. Wait, the jeep will be repaired, you can go then. I'm a doctor, I can't afford to wait, so. Or else I'd have taken the jeep too.'

'It's possible for you to take the truck?'

'Yes, we're used to it.'

'Then I'll get used to it too. If you can, why can't I?' He didn't have an answer to this. He tried to slink away silently, but I called out to him again in desperation.

'Oh Moshai! Please take me along on the ration truck. I have to get there quickly too.'

'Women can't travel on the ration truck. It's a very rough journey. I don't think it will be convenient for you. Dr Lalwani is right, wait a couple of days and take the jeep. The permit might be arranged by then too. You can't go without the permit after all.' The officer spoke with a smile.

'Doesn't the doctor need a permit? Who issues him one?'

'He does. He keeps it with himself; it just has to be renewed. He's the MO of Tawang.'

'MO?' (Not money order, surely!)

'Medical Officer.'

'Then he's my perfect travelling companion. No need to worry in case I fall ill. I'll go with him. Please reserve a seat for me on the ration truck. The permit will be ready by then. Won't it?'

'How can I say? Do you suppose it's in my hands? The ADC is in Itanagar. I can issue the permit only if he instructs me to. He'll be back tomorrow or the day after. Quite soon. Any day now, in fact.'

'Quite soon? Tomorrow? Or the day aaaafter? Threeeeee days? And you're saying any day now?'

'What happened to that phone call?' Dada urged the officer.

'The boy didn't even come back. He should have by now.'

The officer rang the bell, and the boy appeared.

'What about that phone call? What did Itanagar say?'

'Can't get through, Sir.'

'There you are. Can't get through. We tried our best. What can we do if we can't get them on the phone?'

Dada said, 'Of course. Let's go, I'm hungry. Alo's waiting.'

~

Never Shall I Leave You, My Love

Didn't work. We were on our way back. Depressed. Suddenly it struck me, mustn't let the doctor fellow go off. He must be held back.

'Let's go to the guest house, Dada. Let's get hold of that Dr Lalwani.'

'Why? How can he help?'

'Ration truck or jeep, whatever he travels in, I'll travel the same way. Medical officer, after all. I have to make arrangements once I get to Tawang too, don't I? You won't have to worry about me if I can go with him.'

'What if you don't get the permit in time?'

'That would be bad luck. No harm trying.' The doctor was pacing up and down in the veranda of the guest house like a crane. Professor Bose fetched him.

'Come along, let me show you where our house is. You can have a cup of coffee with us. We'll bring you back.'

'Why should I be shown where your house is?'

'What if you go off leaving me behind? If you know where the house is, you can pick me up on the way when you're leaving, even if you can't inform me in advance. It's very urgent. I'm writing something about the Tawang Monastery. I teach at a university. Nomoshkar.'

'Namaskar.'

'Come along then? For a cup of coffee?'

'It's safe for her to travel with you, don't you see?' Dada told him. 'A young woman travelling alone, not a good idea....'

'That's true. But ...'

'You're leaving tomorrow, right? What time?'

'That depends on when the ration truck leaves. Around eleven?'

Might as well ring up Jeep-babu to tell him I won't be going with him. What use would it be to travel just halfway? This was a much better arrangement. All the way.

We were astonished when we telephoned.

Jeep-babu was gone.

He had already left for Bomdila.

'Come to think of it, we didn't see his jeep with the yellow curtains when we passed his house.'

I was deeply hurt. He had our address and phone number. He neither rang nor informed us, and certainly didn't take me along. What if I had been waiting to travel with him? Why do people behave this way?

~

If My Best Efforts Go Unanswered

Sheela Barthakur's husband had promised to help with the permit. We rang him. He too said he couldn't do anything till the ADC returned. I was going from desperate to more desperate.

I had a sudden brainwave. 'Where can we get an Itanagar phone directory, Dada?'

'There, in that drawer.'

'You have one right here? That's enough. Let me try myself.'

'Do you know anyone there?'

'No. Can't I ring if I don't know anyone?'

'Whom will you ring?'

Let's see, someone in the government.'

Shami ran to get the directory. Alo-di was excited too. Whom is she calling now? Dada was beset by worry. The directory yielded no information about who might be in charge of issuing permits. I was hunched over the directory, listening to the running commentary.

'Wild goose chase.' Dada's comment.

'You are crazy, Mashi.' Shami.

'Uff, let her try.' Alo-di had defected to my side. Suddenly my eyes stopped at one particular name. A conversation I had overheard in Jorhat. We had been invited to dinner. Someone from Itanagar was also there. He was telling Vijay Hendrique, the MLA (a friend of ours, whose wife Rani had driven me to

Kaziranga), that a close friend (or relation?) of his was posted in Itanagar as advisor to the lieutenant governor. His name had sounded rather strange—Thound.

Now here was the same name in the directory. Mr Thound, advisor to the lieutenant governor. Must be the same man.

Dial.

Direct to the office of the advisor to the lieutenant governor.

'Hello. This is Thound.'

Pouring as much gravity into my tone as possible, I said in a voice as heavy as lead, 'Nomoshkar. This is Dr Nabaneeta Dev Sen from Tezpur. I am here from Calcutta to participate in the Assam Women's Literature Conference in Jorhat.'

'Oh, Dr Dev Sen? I was listening to an interview of yours on Guwahati Radio just yesterday. When did you come to Tezpur?'

It was my turn to be astonished. What was this? I was embarrassed now for having introduced myself as Dr Dev Sen to impress him.

'I enjoyed your interview. You are absolutely right. I read the interview in *Janmabhoomi* too. You can read Ahomiya, can't you?'

'Only a little.' (I was back to being a mouse by now.)

'Tell me why you called. What can I do for you?'

'Oh yes. I'd like to visit Tawang Monastery. But the ADC is not here, he's in Itanagar. They won't issue an inner line permit without him. I'm getting a lift tomorrow with the MO, so I thought....'

'Not to worry. Give me half an hour. What's your phone number?'

'...'

'I read your lecture too in the papers. Very pleased to make your acquaintance. Are you planning to write about Tawang Monastery?'

'Yes, sort of, you know what I mean. Oh yes, I heard about you from Vijay Hendrique, so....'

'That's right, how are they?'

'They're very well. It was Rani who ...'

'Very well, have a good trip to Tawang Monastery....'

Within half an hour there was a phone call from the ADC's office. Dr Sen's permit should be collected by five o'clock. Dr Sen should come personally, she has to sign.

I danced off. Shami was bursting with pride. And Dada was looking as though it was all his handiwork.

Shami looked as though it was his.

Only Alo-di was saying, 'Didn't I tell you she's no ordinary woman? Let her do things exactly as she wants. She's been to the Kumbh.'

~

I Must Go, I *Must* Go

By evening Sheela Barthakur's double-breasted green over-coat had arrived. So had Ila-di's father-in-law's monkey cap, gloves, and muffler. Alo-di pulled out Dada's sleeveless sli-pover and Shami's full-sleeved pullover and socks. Then we went out to buy shoes. Socks too, two pairs of a nylon-wool blend. 'Export-quality' keds from Bata. I came back home in a state of euphoria and began to pack.

Alo-di, Ila-di, and Shami were excited. Dada was not, and hovered over us with a listless expression. Brightening sud-denly, he announced, 'You'll need a medical check-up in the morning. You can go only if the doctor says, yes, you're fit to travel. Not otherwise.'

Fresh trouble. Health has always been my weak point. I wasn't allowed to join the NCC for being underweight. And now the body is the ye olde temple of disease. The less the doctor knoweth, the better.

'Look, I have a couple of chronic illnesses. Nothing to get perturbed about. If you check my pressure you might find the diastolic to be a hundred and the systolic anywhere between a hundred and ten and a hundred and forty. I have a medicine named Brinerdin. I'll take it twice a day.

'Plus if you check my chest with your stethoscope you'll hear whistling sounds of asthmatic spasms. It's nothing. I'm used to it. I take steroids every day, asthma pills too. I take care.

'Besides, I have a slightly ischemic heart. But then, almost every adult in Calcutta has the same heart condition. I have Sorbitrate. So, Doctor, whatever you may find, you must understand that this is my normal functioning condition—my natural state of health. You can't compare me to others. I go to work every day with all this, why can't I go on a holiday? Can anyone withstand everything? I can. I'm very hardy.

'In addition, I have a slightly rheumatic shoulder, and I sometimes get migraines. But then I have medicines for those too. I won't yield without a fight, you see. I have all my weapons. Even Chloroquine for malaria, Enteroquinol for diarrhoea. The entire medicinal tree. Unless I'm gored by a mad bull ...'

Alo-di couldn't stand it any longer.

'Enough. Stop the train. Let him examine you. You're wasting his time.'

The doctor was a Bengali. He listened to my speech calmly. Then, examining the patient with great care, he laughed.

'Right on every count. BP hundred by one-twenty-five. I'd have been worried if you hadn't warned me. Half a Brinerdin at once. It shouldn't be at hundred. That's the reason for the ischemia. There are spasms too, but not alarming. Keep taking the medicine. But since you're going to Tawang alone, I'd suggest taking the steroid three times a day for the sake of safety. You can taper it down when you're back. Do you have a spray?'

'I do, but no extras. Might run out of it. Imported, you see. Didn't have too many.'

'Buy a Neo-epinine, take a Brovon spray along, and keep extra supplies of all the medicines since you insist on going. Not that I'm pronouncing you healthy....'

'In that case I'd have to be on medical leave round the year....'

'Go if you must, but given your state of health, it isn't right to take this risk. It's reassuring that you'll have a doctor travelling with you. But remember not to climb all the way at one go. Reaching a high altitude too quickly can affect the functioning of the brain. You must take a break on the way. That's one of the reasons we lost the war with the Chinese.'

'What do you mean?'

'I mean that General so-and-so was so anxious that he drove non-stop at breakneck speed to Tawang. The body cannot adjust to climbing to such an altitude so quickly. His brain was affected. But it wasn't obvious. The decisions he took and the orders he issued were crazy. Self-destructive and replete with wrong judgements. No one knew it then, but later it was found out that medically he was absolutely unfit.'

'My god!'

'Stop for breaks, Nabaneeta, stop for breaks,' said Dada anxiously. 'Don't travel non-stop. Even if that man wants to, tell him the story of the general. All right?'

'He's a doctor himself. He will never climb non-stop,' said Alo-di.

I had already rung Dr Lalwani to tell him that I had got my permit. On his part he had let me know that neither of the two jeeps had been repaired and that the ration truck was still being loaded. It would leave in the evening.

It was time to buy medicines now. Dada's car was available round the clock. Really, such care, so much love, all the solicitousness—as though I really was Dada's own sister. Years have passed, but the memory of that warmth has not diminished in the least. Alo-di was charming, and just as efficient. Hasan and Husain were well-matched. Both were extremely sociable, full of wit. Alo-di had given a secret name to the short curtains that we middle-class Bengalis use for our windows:

bodice curtains. Bare on top and below, covered in the middle. Like a blouse designed like a choli, hiding nothing in the room. She said it after swearing me to secrecy, however. I'm sure she'll be piqued to hear I've published it. I spent a very short time in Tezpur, but my relationship with Dada, Alo-di, and Shami was like a bond of many years.

The day passed in chatting and heightened excitement. I rang my mother in Calcutta to give her the news. 'I'll be a week late—I'm going for a trip outside Tezpur, to Arunachal. Don't worry, all right?'

I told Dada to book a plane ticket to Calcutta for me. I was leaving in the evening for Tawang with seven days to spare. All the way to the McMahon Line. Along the same Lhasa–Tawang Road which the Chinese had taken. Ever since I had heard Rita Gupta in Shillong talk about the monastery with its magnificent collection of manuscripts, I had been dying to go there. And now I really was.

Tucking Ila-di's father-in-law's cap and gloves and muffler into the pockets of Sheela's coat, placing Shami and his father's sweaters on top of my other clothes in the suitcase, and drawing my shawl around myself, I set off gingerly with my luggage and a prayer on my lips to the place where the truck was supposed to be waiting. When I reached, good god! A huge, intimidating lorry. The kind that mounts pavements to run over people sleeping on them. For some reason I had assumed that a truck would be a covered military vehicle.

I can't say I wasn't rattled at the sight of this open-backed lorry. Although it was in just such lorries that I used to accompany the idol of Durga to the immersion. But this wasn't really an uncovered vehicle. It was stacked as high as the first floor of a building. Innumerable sacks, bags, and paper cartons. In addition, entire steel cupboards. And a good deal of wicker furniture. On which sat baskets of chickens of different sizes, covered with webbing. They were expressing extreme disapproval with loud clucks. How would I clamber over all this, and where would Dr Lalwani sit, for that matter?

'What on earth is this thing? How are people supposed to sit in there? No, no, no. You are not going in this. Impossible.' Dada shook his head continuously from left to right and back. He had come to see me off with his favourite grandniece in his arms (his niece's daughter), along with Alo-di. I will never forget the way he shook his head. I would have shaken my head too in his place.

'No, no, no. This is madness—it's absolutely stuffed. How can you even get in there?'

Alo-di said in surprise, 'And it has no roof either. Even if there had been space, I'd never allow you into a truck with no overhead cover. You'll catch a chill and get pneumonia. I had expected some sort of roof. How can anyone travel in this enormous cargo lorry? You can't go. Let's go back.' Alo-di lodged a strong protest.

I too was nervous.

Indeed. The spirit was willing, but the flesh was weak. There wasn't the slightest space in there. Even the chickens were annoyed. How could I sit on top of this monument of material? I'd fall off as soon as the truck started to move.

I had no reasonable logic to counter Dada and Alo-di with. Everything they were saying was justified.

I felt angry and dejected. This meant I couldn't leave today.

All right. The jeep was being repaired. Let it regain its health. I would go, I would certainly go. If not in this one, then in another one.

Where had the doctor gone? Must have disappeared in some other vehicle because he couldn't get into this one.

They're all the same. No one thinks of me. Neither god nor idols.

Suddenly the doctor appeared at a distance, looking shy. He showed no sign of having recognized me.

Dada went up to him, looking worried.

'Where will she sit? This is loaded.'

'The seating is inside.' The doctor was taciturn.

'Inside what?' Dada trained a penetrating gaze to the base of the mountain of material. Checking for a cave.

'Next to the driver.'

I hadn't noticed all this while. Of course, there was a covered portion up front. Where the driver, cleaner, and all sat. Could more people fit in there? Let me check how much room there was. Trying to peep in, I realized how high a lorry is. The driver was sitting on a throne. A long distance from the ground. The base of the door was level with my head. There were three rungs to climb. They were arranged vertically, like a ladder, not a staircase. Very difficult to negotiate. It would be impossible to get in unless someone hauled me up by the hand. There were no handles or anything to hold on to while climbing. Dada opened the door himself, craning his neck for a view. Someone was sitting inside. The driver, perhaps. Could be the cleaner too. I stepped forward to hand him my suitcase. He took it, looking as though he was expecting me. Stretching my right hand, I said, unnecessarily brusquely, *'Meherbani karke hamara haath pakarke upar khinch lijiyega zara.'* (Please pull me up by my hand; lead me by the hand, my friend!) He leant out and held out his own. Accepted my hand, so to speak. I held on to it firmly and climbed carefully up the rungs. Once I was up there I abandoned my gravity, saying with a reassured smile, 'Thank you, ji.'

Returning my smile he said in Hindi, 'It's too high for you. Be careful when you get off.'

Done. The teamwork would continue. That smile had sealed the fact that we were a team. Confidently, I scanned, surveyed, and sized up the seats. Not too bad. Like the bench seats on old buses. Long enough for four or five people. Pretty good.

Dada and Alo-di stood outside with their grandniece. Anxiously.

'Well, what's it like? Comfortable?'

'Very comfortable, Alo-di, please don't worry.'

'When do you leave?'

'Anytime now,' answered the driver.

'In fifteen minutes. Two people are yet to come. It'll leave as soon as they arrive.'

'Then we'll leave now,' said Alo-di. 'The baby has to eat at six. Take care. Take your medicines on time.'

'You must stop on the way. Don't forget.'

'Be careful.'

'Don't be late coming back.'

'We'll be worried. You'll be alone.'

'Relax.' I wasn't going alone. I never go alone anywhere. That's what's interesting.

'Don't worry. I'll be back on time.'

Those who have no one still have you. Why doesn't anyone remember this wonderful truth? Rajanikanta used to say things simply, without poetic emotion. It appeals to me.

Oh! Alone. Alone. Alone.

The refrain really does make the heart feel alone.

Not alone? How?

Is there anyone in the world who isn't alone? Even Siamese twins are alone at one point. We talk about the two of us, the four of us, the ten of us. True. But that's us. What about me? How many am I? I'm not the two of me. 'I' implies alone.

There's loneliness wherever I am. Being the only child, I have been at the receiving end of this invective of 'alone' since birth.

And now there's a new round of admonishments for being 'alone' because I don't run a stereotypical household.

It's all very well to say all this to me, but are there two of you?

You're alone too.

I'm alone. So are you.

This is a grammatical fact. Loneliness is the fundamental condition.

But I'm not alone.

Those who have no one still have you. Who knows the truth of this better than me?

Dada and Alo-di left with their grandniece. With the arrival of the other two passengers, the doctor got in too. Our lorry, sorry, truck, turned on its headlights—like a searchlight, the beams spread out into the distance. A couple of incense sticks had been stuck into a stand. They were lit.

A piece of thin, white cloth was wrapped around a stick bent like a garland. The five of us were sitting side by side. It was not at all uncomfortable. My coat and suitcase were next to me. Six people could have fitted in. Of course, none of us was fat. I was worried about the smell of the incense aggravating my asthma because I'm allergic to incense smoke. A notorious sinner if there ever was one. There was another sharp smell from the other side—a little less holy. I didn't have a taste for this either. It was making me nauseous. How many days in this stench? How many hours? How many endless moments? This was going to be a problem. I'd give it a little longer. Once the truck started moving, the wind might blow away both the aroma and the odour.

Even as I was wondering the truck blew its horn and set off. May the goddess protect us. My Gurudas-dada would have said, *Jai*. Whose victory? Over what? Nothing like that. Simply victory. The winner knew very well whose victory it was and would claim it.

~

Mr Sen and Mrs Sen

'Namaste. *Aapka shubhnam?*'

It seemed best to begin with Hindi. Pan-Indian language. And definitely the truck driver's. I started with the young man on my right. He was nineteen or twenty.

'Myla.'

'What do you do?'

'I'm the cleaner.'

'Are you Ahomiya?'

'No. Nepali.'

'Nepali. I see. And your name, driver sahib?'

'Ji, Manchand.'

'You're not Ahomiya either?'

(My Hindi was depleted by now.)

'*Ji nahin.* I'm from Rajputana. I'm a Jat.'

'Such a long way from Rajputana?'

'What's the alternative? Have to eat, have to earn a living.'

'Have you been working here a long time?'

'Yes. I have an Assamese wife. I've set up home here.' The young man turned to me and smiled. A lovely, dazzling smile.

'Excellent. But don't you miss Rajputana?' Manchand smiled again. Glittering teeth.

'I visit sometimes. My parents live there. My brother too. I send money home every month.'

My next question was to the person on my left. He was the one responsible for filling the cab with a foul stench. His toddy had kept pace with the incense. I was terrified that he would drop off any moment with his head on my shoulder. So it was absolutely essential to keep him awake. And what to do with this stink? Clearing my throat, I began.

'Namaste, ji.'

'Nnnnmaste. Grr....'

'What is your name?'

'Grrra....'

'Tell the lady your name, she's asking,' Myla said loudly, laughing. Very amused.

'Nnnname? My name is Mr Sen. Yours?' He answered, opening one eye.

'Mrs Sen.'

'What!' Both his eyes flew open. He no longer seemed drunk. He had an air of *Did I hear right?* Perturbed.

'What did you say your name is?'

'Mrs Sen.'

'Mrs Sen? Are you a Bengali?'

'I am.'

'A Vaidya?'

'Half, actually. Not by birth, but by marriage.'

'Same thing,' he said, switching to Bengali with an East Bengal accent. Your new caste by way of marriage is what you are now. Good. Mrs Sen, Mr Sen. Mr Sen, Mrs Sen. Very good.'

My god! I'd been told that drunk people get over their drunkenness when given important tasks. So I told him, 'Mr Sen, I'm very allergic to smoke. The smoke from the incense sticks will give me asthma. Can you find a way to put them out?'

'Impossible! These are there to protect us. So many dangers on hill roads. The joss sticks keep perils away. They mustn't be put out. I can't do it.'

So I was forced to seek the doctor's help. I made the same plea, this time in English. And was given the same answer in English. The doctor added something more.

'You'd better sit on this side, by the window. The incense sticks are in front of the driver, the smoke won't travel all this way. You'll get some fresh air too. Change your seat when the truck stops. They'll go out soon though.'

Without paying attention to that assurance, I said, 'If Mr Sen could also shift to that side next to the driver, and Myla and you sat between them and me, both the smells will be at a distance. I can't stand the other one either.'

'Sorry, Mrs Sen, sorry,' said Mr Sen. Which meant he understood English quite well. 'I had no idea there would be a female passenger, else I wouldn't have had a drink today. Women never travel here, except for families.'

'Meaning?'

'Meaning families travel on this route often. Maybe the husband has a business or a job at Bomdila or Jamiri or Dirajgong or Rupa. When they're travelling with their families, the ladies and babies sit here with the driver. But I've rarely seen a lady travelling alone. I can't remember even one.'

The more he spoke, the stronger the odour grew. I had no choice but to say, 'Could you stop for a minute, Manchand-ji? I have to change seats. The bad smell is making me....'

'Of course. In a short while. There'll be a lay-by soon.'

The truck stopped. I changed to a seat by the window. Next to me sat the doctor, then Myla, Mr Sen, and Manchand. Getting out and then back in using the notches cut into the side for the feet needed considerable dexterity. Manchand helped me. He had got off from his side of the truck. He was the one who had helped me climb in. Myla showed me the slots with a torch. There we were, a wonderful family. I didn't feel lonely at all. Who says I travel alone? Never. With family. Always with family. A person can have more than one family, after all.

The truck stopped. Mr Sen said there was a ration shop here where they had to deliver supplies. We could have a cup of tea meanwhile. There was a tea shop across the road. I went to the tiny stationery shop first to buy a torch and batteries. Not having a torch is a problem, for one has to depend on others for some light. This shop probably didn't get strangely dressed city-bred women customers too often. There was a crowd of little boys and girls. It was a brilliant shop. Hair oil and soap, slates and pencils, notebooks and ink, biscuits and lozenges, all sorts of plastic things, gunny bags, school bags, pots and pans, knives and scissors, stoves and lanterns … you name it, they had it. Even bedcovers and lungis and sweaters. I'd never seen such a refined department store in an eight-by-ten-foot space.

Coming out of the shop I found Manchand, Myla, and Mr Sen busy unloading bulky sacks. Where had the doctor disappeared to?

There he was.

With a glass of tea. Doctor Beanpole was standing in the dark.

I joined him, with a glass of tea of my own.

At once he proceeded towards the lorry absently, still holding the glass.

What was going on? Where was he running off? Was he running away from me? What fun.

Should I follow him? Frighten him? No, never mind. Let him go wherever he likes. I'll have my tea right here.

Let him have his in peace over there.

~

Elephant! Cheetah! Jackal!

We were done with the tea.

Manchand was blowing the horn. The doctor came back to return the glass. He had no choice. I struck up a conversation.

'When will we stop again?'

'I don't know,' said the doctor, placing his glass on the counter.

We went back into the truck, and set off.

'No stops now,' said Mr Sen. 'We're entering the forest, you see. You can see lots of animals.'

'Really? What kind?'

My head was full of the Kaziranga experience.

'All kinds. Herds of elephants, cheetahs, monkeys, rhinos, deer, bears, rabbits, plenty, plenty of them.'

'Will we be able to see them?'

'Of course. They'll be caught in the headlights, you'll see. So many animals. I'll point them out if you like....'

'You will? Yes, please do.' I was ecstatic.

Soon, he began to yell.

'Elephant! There! Look!' Following his pointing finger, I indeed saw an elephant that had come out of the jungle to rub its trunk against a cement gate on the side of the highway.

'There's one on your side too,' said Mr Sen.

On my side? Yes, he was right! There was indeed another one on this side of the gate. In the same charming pose. What was going on?

Ah.

Cement figures.

Statues of elephants. Enormous. Painted.

In the darkness of the night they did look like the real thing.

'Ha ha ha what fun! You've been fooled, Mrs Sen!'

'Heh. Yes, very funny.'

(Funny my foot.)

Neither Myla nor Manchand talked much. The doctor's lips were sealed. It would have been best if Mr Sen had remained silent, but he was the one doing all the talking. The man seemed a decent sort. After his intermediate exams he began travelling in search of work, even joining the army. He was from north Bengal, and had settled down in Jorhat. His wife was Ahomiya. He had had one in north Bengal too, a Bengali woman. They had even had a son, but he had left them. Who knows what happened to them. Parents? They had died when he was still a child. His Ahomiya wife was very nice. They had two daughters, one of whom was married. She was from a previous marriage, however, from his second wife's first husband. Mr Sen was the father of the other daughter, who was a schoolgirl. Yes, they were very happy. He had married a widow. Her first husband had been a soldier who died in the war against China. The beautiful young widow was in dire straits with her child. She had brought a rhythm into Mr Sen's vagabond-like existence. He had left his first wife and son a long time ago; his life was completely different by then. Not a happy one at all.

'I was irresponsible by nature. My uncle made me get married. It was a mistake. I was not ready for it.'

As if he was quite ready now. I was angry at first, but then I told myself, perhaps he was. Drinking did not amount to debauchery. Clearly he loved his wife and daughters very much.

We kept driving, he kept talking, I kept listening. It was all going well. But suddenly he asked, 'What does your husband do, Mrs Sen? Is he posted in Tawang?'

He was right. Considering my eagerness to get to Tawang, people could well imagine that someone was waiting anxiously for me there. What should I say now?

There was an opportunity here to fib. I could easily say that Mr Sen had disappeared twenty years ago and had turned up as a lama at the Tawang Monastery. Or that he had been posted at Tawang since the war with China, and that there had been no news since then. Or, yes, quite right, he'll be there to welcome me.

But where was I headed? Where was this truck taking me, to what address? I had no idea. Even as I pondered I heard myself say, 'Mr Sen lives in England.'

'England? What's his line of business? Does he run a restaurant? Lots of Bengalis in that field.'

Seizing the chance to change the subject, I said, 'Oh yes, it's full of Bengalis from Sylhet and Chittagong. Of course, most of them are Bangladeshi now. Indian restaurants are very popular.'

'Hasn't your husband ever taken you to England? Have you been to London?'

'Oh yes, several times.'

'Very good. There must be more Bengali women in England.'

'Lots. Hordes of them.'

'We've done nothing with our lives.'

'Why do you say that?'

'Haven't even seen the world. Frogs in the well.'

'That's not true. You've met many kinds of people, experienced different ways of living, done so many different things in so many different places. Yours is quite an unusual life.'

'But I've never worked on a ship. I always wanted to be a sailor. Never got the chance. There—a cheetah.'

'What? Where?'

'Cheetah! There! Running away. You can see the eyes. Look. Eyes.' He was right. A pair of green eyes. Some sort of small creature raced away, and then whirled round suddenly, its eyes blazing in the darkness.

'That's a cheetah?'

'Of course. Didn't I tell you there are leopards here? Deer too. And bears. Huge.'

Now I shouted too:

'There! Did you see that? A leopard! Why can't any of you see it? How strange!'

Vastly perturbed at the lack of interest of my companions, I nudged the unmoved doctor sitting by my side. The sudden shove made the silent doctor break into speech.

'What leopard? That's a jackal. Leopards don't come near humans.'

'But he said it was.'

'He's had too much to drink. You don't see too many animals on this road, barring jackals and rabbits. A few deer sometimes, that's true. Monkeys? One of two. Elephants have been spotted now and then, though they seldom venture this side. Bears? Never. Bison? No idea. Rhinos? Never. Look, he's talking nonsense.'

Anger had loosened the doctor's tongue. I might as well use the opportunity to chat him up. Now that I had managed to get him to talk.

'Where are you from, Doctor?'

'Baroda. It used to be Sindh. Which is now part of Pakistan.'

'Where did you get your degree?'

'Bombay.'

'How long ago?'

'About three years.'

'That's all? And how long have you been working here?'

'Two years.'

'Is that all? Whom do you have back home?'

'Everyone.'

'Who's everyone?'

'Parents, grandparents, brothers, and sisters.'

'Why didn't you study further instead of taking a job so soon....'

'Oh, I will. Let me save some money. I can't take my father's money, can I? I'm not clever enough for a scholarship. So this job. I'm saving. Three more years and I'll be in America.'

'Why America?'

'I'd rather go there. England is old-fashioned.'

'Are Indian degrees recognized in the US?'

'They are. There's no problem with higher studies. You can study at a teaching hospital while you work.'

'You seem to have found out everything. All that's left now is to actually go there.'

With a shy smile the doctor fell silent. He didn't ask me a single question, only answered mine. As though he was appearing at an interview. Even Mr Sen had not pressed home the question about 'What does your husband do?' He was furious with the doctor for saying, 'He is talking nonsense', and for turning his leopards into jackals. He had become a Trappist monk.

The incense had long burnt down to ashes. But the smoke persisted. Myla lit cigarettes at regular intervals and held them to Manchand's lips. He was smoking too.

Even cigarette smoke makes me wheeze. But not tonight. Both the windows were open. The night wind whistled across our faces, boring through the truck. It was cold, but not freezing. It was refreshing. I was drowsy. Placing my elbow on the window frame, I tried to rest my head on it and sleep. Sheela Barthakur's coat and my bag lay between the doctor and me. A shawl was enough to keep warm.

Myla was humming a Nepali tune. It worked like a lullaby. Weren't any of them going to eat? No dinner? I was hungry.

~

Madras Hotel

'Wake up, Memsahib, wake up. We're at Bhalukpang. You have to show them your permit.'

Grabbing my bag, I held out my hand. Someone took it in the darkness, and shone a torch on the steps. I climbed down, thinking, why not climb down backwards, like a ladder, instead of making it so difficult for myself? There was a small handle inside the cabin I could hold on to.

Presenting my permit at the military checkpoint, I discovered that they knew Doctor Giraffe quite well.

'Hello, yaar.' 'Hi, Doctor.' And so on. The army boys weren't very old either. All of them living it up in camp.

'No dinner for you, Doctor?'

'I'll eat here. There's the Madrasi restaurant.'

He was right! Dressed casually in a shirt and a half-dhoti, a smiling, enterprising soul from the distant south had indeed started a restaurant for idlis and dosas here at this dangerous checkpoint on the north-east frontier. A signboard hung in front of us with the legend, Madras Hotel. Benches and tables were laid out inside. The price list was scrawled on a blackboard—idli, curry, rice, lassi, coffee. Not expensive at all. Cheaper than in Calcutta, in fact. But hauling all this stuff here was no joke. Running a southern kitchen meant importing cooks from south India—there was the train fare to be paid. I realized that India's future lay in the south.

Sitting next to each other, we ate the same piping hot mas- ala dosa and drank south Indian coffee. Delicious. But Dr Giraffe didn't utter a word. As though he didn't even know me. All the shyness and hesitation in the world seemed to bear down on him like a soldier with a bayonet when it came to a conversation with me.

Settling our respective bills, we returned together in silence to the lorry. The vehicle resumed its journey.

You had to hand it to Madras Hotel! I saw two or three men from the south working busily, some working, some serving, some keeping the accounts and counting money. I couldn't keep myself from asking, 'Are all of you from Madras?' I was addressing the man counting the money. Probably the owner. The answer came, accompanied by a sweet smile, 'No.'

I was astonished. Not from Madras! Where, then?

'Kerala. We're from Trivandrum.' I wasn't surprised this time. 'That explains it. Kerala.'

The people of Kerala know how to get about. Calcutta had always been full of nurses and typists from Kerala. I'd even read about nurses from Kerala being sent to Germany and England these days. Of late the Gulf countries were being flooded with people from Kerala. The men from the state were taking up jobs in droves in Dubai—and it was raining money in Kerala's towns and villages. The land was changing, in appearance and in character. And in comparison to Dubai, north-east India was a cakewalk.

'But why Madras Hotel? Why not Kerala Café or Trivandrum Hotel?'

'No one knows those places. Madras is a big city. The south means Madras to most people. The more popular name, you see?'

'I see.'

I could clearly see that development was inevitable for Kerala. Despite its imminent collapse, Bengal wouldn't be woken up by even a thousand Keralas. After all, Kerala was an educated state. India's only fully literate state. Naturally. There were government libraries in every village. I had seen for myself how ordinary people went to the well-lit libraries in the evening to read the newspapers, magazines, and books. Never mind villages, was it a sight we saw even in our cities? We preferred to visit our neighbours or watch the TV.

~

Late at Night, a Crescent Moon

The truck continued on the mountain road after Bhalukpang. A river seemed to be racing alongside us. The night was no longer as dark as before. The moon had risen. We all know that everything—mountains, the sea, even a vast field—looks bewitching in the moonlight. But that night, in the light of the mountain moon, the road seemed to be steeped in an unbelievable beauty.

The moon spins its own magic in the hills, especially if it's accompanied on one side by a truck filled with sleepy but careful eyes racing along a twisting, turning road, and on the other by mysterious forests flashing past while unnamed mountain streams wound around the curves—a supernatural scene, all told. It could well turn us mad, even a battlefield-bound army general. Who knows whether it was that kind of night. How the moon played hide and seek, how it ran about everywhere! Now on the mountain peak, now between the trees, now in the arms of the river, now in the sky above a turn in the road—havoc! Thank goodness it wasn't I who was driving but Manchand! At least the truck was hurtling along without paying attention to any of this. The mischiefs of the moon hadn't been able to distract it. It had seen all this far too often.

~

Funeroo Coming Your Way Tonight

The truck stopped. It was around 11.30 at night. Mr Sen finally broke his injured silence.

'We're staying the night here.'

'Ah. Where will we sleep?'

'How should I know where you will sleep?'

Was there a genuine note of despair in Mr Sen's voice?

'Oh no, I'm not talking about myself,' I said, embarrassed. 'Where will all of you sleep?'

'I'm sleeping in the lorry. We have so much of our supplies in here.'

'Where in the lorry?'

'On this seat, obviously. Once all of you have got off.'

'I see. What about Manchand? And Myla?'

'The driver will sleep here too. There's a bunk here that can be let down.'

'And Myla?'

'He has a relative in that shop there. That's where he'll sleep.'

He pointed to a building. It was an elongated structure, with two or three rooms. Packed with people. Very noisy.

'What sort of shop is it?'

'A hotel of some kind.'

'I can stay there then.'

'You won't be able to. No arrangement for ladies.'

'Well then? Will the doctor sleep there?'

'No, the doctor's going to IB. That's where they always stay.'

I discovered the doctor ambling off somewhere. In the darkness I spotted a house in that direction, a one-storeyed building, with a gate leading into a garden of sorts in front. Some jeeps were parked inside. This hotel with the temporary roof was on its right. There were people outside as well, sitting on cots and eating out of hand-held bowls. All of this was on the left side of the road. On the right was a ravine.

Now that the truck had fallen silent a different sound had become audible. The roar of a waterfall close by.

'What's this IB business?'

'You don't know what IB is! How strange.'

Mr Sen seemed to be struggling for words.

'You've been to England, and you don't know IB?'

'Intelligence Branch? What do doctors have to do with it?'

I was genuinely worried now. These areas were dangerous. Who knew what sort of spy this damned doctor was? Maybe that was why he wouldn't speak. IB connections. What should I do now? Meanwhile, I could hear Mr Sen speaking.

'I don't know about intelligence or anything, Madam, IB stands for Inspection Bungalow. You are the first educated person I have met in my life who doesn't know what IB is.'

An extremely irritated Mr Sen got off the truck and left with a glum expression, just about holding himself back from saying 'Shame on you!' and from spitting loudly.

I got off too, wondering what I should do, when Manchand returned.

'Go to IB, Memsahib, you'll get a room there.'

'What are you people going to do now? Will you eat?'

With a shy smile, and scratching his head in embarrass-ment, Manchand said, 'May I be honest? We're going to have a little drink. I don't touch a drop while driving. Our gods have forbidden us. Drink at night after you're done driving. That is all right. Only tea during the day, nothing more. Hill driving is dangerous. If you drink, you're dead.'

He seemed to have had his first drink already. Manchand continued, 'I came to tell you that we'll start at five in the morning. Please be on time. We won't wait. Please tell Doctor Sahib too.'

'Oh please don't leave without me. How will I go on if you do?'

'You'll get plenty of transport. Lots of trucks pass this way all day.'

~

The Night Leaves Us Behind

The doctor was striding back towards us. I went forward. As soon as he saw me he did an about turn and started walking towards the bungalow. So did I. I had no choice. I would have to get myself a room in the bungalow, after all. The doctor stopped eventually, and then turned to me and began to talk. This was the first time he was addressing me without being prompted.

'The chowkidar isn't responding. There are people in the bungalow.'

'Let's look for him. Where does he live?'

'Right there, at the back.'

There was a row of small buildings behind the bungalow.

'Chowkidar! Chowkidar!' We shouted in unison, banging on the doors.

A young girl emerged. A girl from the hills.

'The chowkidar isn't here.'

'Where has he gone?'

'There, to the hotel.'

'Let's go to the hotel, Doctor.'

'Do you think we'll find him there?'

'She's saying he's there, why shouldn't we find him? Isn't he supposed to be on duty at the bungalow? Let's fetch him.'

The doctor seemed far too soft-natured and gentle. He walked around in embarrassed circles outside the hotel. Eventually I was the one who had to call out loudly.

'Is the chowkidar here? Is the IB chowkidar here? The IB chowkidar?'

'*Ji huzoor.*'

A man appeared in a minute. Complete with a salute. When he had taken a good look at us, he said, 'Oh, it's Dagdaar Sahib.'

His attention seemed to dwindle.

'You'll have to check at the hotel. See if you can get a room.'

'Meaning?'

'All the rooms are full. Have you seen the number of jeeps? The MLA is here with his people.'

'Not even one room available?'

'Not even one.'

'All of them taken?'

'A ... ll of them.'

'What do we do then?'

'I told you. Check at the hotel. You're bound to get a room.'

The doctor looked worried.

He fell silent.

My turn.

'The drawing room is vacant, isn't it?'

'The drawing room?' The chowkidar looked at us in surprise. 'Yes, it's vacant.'

'Very well. Unlock it for me.'

'But that room is never....'

'Or you could call the MLA, I'll talk to him. Let his people vacate a room.'

'Call the MLA? But memsahib, he fell asleep long ago. How can I wake him up? The drawing room will be better ...'

'Yes, that will do.'

'But there's no bed....'

'Never mind. There must be chairs and a table. A sofa or a couch?'

'There are.'

'Let's go and take a look. Come, Doctor.'

The room wasn't very large, but not small either. On the bigger side, in fact. Half of it was in use as a living room; the other half had a huge dining table with several chairs arranged around it. The living area had wicker chairs and a sofa. It was impossible to sleep on that sofa. Two seats, sunken like drawwells. Suddenly an evil idea popped up in my head.

'Come with me, Chowkidar.'

'Where, Memsahib?'

'To the hotel. Just come.'

There were a few cots laid out outside the hotel. Several drunkards were sitting on them, drinking. They seemed to have eaten there too, as the bowls lying around suggested. I said sternly, 'Kindly vacate this cot. It is needed in the IB. Get rid of the bowls quickly.'

The drunkards leapt to their feet and deposited the bowls inside. Three of them and the chowkidar proceeded to take one of the cots to the IB. Leading the way solemnly, I helped them place the cot in the drawing room. I hadn't expected it to be so easy. Doctor Beanpole was surveying the transfer operations from a distance. The drunkards went back to the hotel. They didn't care for tips, they were a free race. The chowkidar said, 'Can I make your bed, Memsahib?' I was astonished. Was I going to get a bed made for me too? Gravely I replied, 'Yes. Double blanket, double sheets, double pillows. Do you have a mattress?'

'No mattress. I'll put in two extra blankets.'

What you might call luxurious sleeping arrangements were made in a moment.

'Two rupees, bedding charge.'

Handing him a five rupee note, I said, '*Bahut shukriya*. Thank you. Now can you get me a cup of tea? And put a lantern in the room.'

Now the doctor spoke up.

'Will I get a room at the hotel, Chowkidar?'

'If you ask for one, why not?' I felt a stab of pity. I really should offer to help.

'Such a large table there. Why don't you lie down on it? Can't he make a bed for you on it?'

'I have my own bedding.'

'Where is it?'

'In the truck.'

'Get it then and go to sleep.'

'In this room?'

'Where will you get another one?'

'But ... in the same room?'

'So what? You became a doctor three years ago, and I became one thirteen years ago. I'm old enough to be your father.'

'You're a doctor too? How strange. Why didn't you say so all this while?'

'I'm a doctor too, but not a medical one. Still, no harm addressing me as Dr Sen. Now get your bedding. There's nothing to fear. I have two grown-up daughters like you. (One was thirteen then, and the other, nine.)

'Of course not, who's afraid?' The doctor brought his bedding and deposited it on the table. But he didn't lay it out. He kept sitting. The chowkidar said, 'I'm lighting the stove. Who wants tea?'

The doctor said, 'I do.'

The chowkidar arranged for a bathroom too when I asked. One of the bathrooms being used by the MLA's party could also be entered from the corridor. The chowkidar opened it for me, and put a light inside. No problem.

I slipped out for a walk while the tea was being made. The sound of the waterfall rang in my ears, in my heart. There was bright moonlight. The road was deserted. Not a soul anywhere. The trees stood still against the mountain, taking in the moon's caresses. I walked along the stream, following the sound of the waterfall. The air was redolent with the fragrance of wild flowers. Of course, the moonlight had turned all of them white. The mountain stream was flowing far below. The sound was even farther away. Strange insects swarmed on the leaves, emitting a variety of sounds. Even the noise from the hotel had faded—there was just the sound of the waterfall, and the buzzing of insects. It was all so wonderfully serene. I was really enjoying my walk, as well as the echoes of my footsteps. Walking around a curve in the road, I paused for a minute at the edge, bending over for a glimpse of the stream. And then ... my heart leapt into my mouth, my limbs froze in fear. I was no longer walking—how could my footsteps still be echoing then? Was it a ghost? Another wave of fear hit me the very next moment. Why should it be a ghost? It must be someone else. Someone else. Someone else. Here on this desolate mountain, at 12.30 in the morning by the stream—someone was coughing. There it was! A distinct cough.

'Who's there?'

I bellowed suddenly. *'Kaun hai?'*

'Lalwani.' Doctor Beanpole came up to me. He was very perturbed for some reason, panting.

'Are you mad? Are you crazy? Neurotic?'

'Why?'

'Who walks out like this at this hour in this deserted area? What a dangerous lady! Come to IB, there's a bathroom there.'

'Of course there's a bathroom there. Who needs a bathroom?'

'What did you come here for then?'

'No particular reason. I came for a walk. To find out where the sound of the waterfall was coming from. Is the tea ready?'

'Who knows whether the tea is ready? I've been following you from a distance, not knowing the purpose of your walk. The sound of the waterfall! It's two miles away. *You are certainly a crazy lady! My god!'*

I had never seen or heard the words crazy and lady next to each other. They were very well suited. Crazy lady. Of course, Mrs Gandhi could also have been described that way a year ago, during the Emergency, but not me. I was not crazy, and definitely not a lady.

'Come, let's go back....' Beanpole sneezed loudly.

'Don't you have a sweater? It's quite cold. Why are you dressed in nothing but a shirt?'

'Where was the time to put a sweater on? When you went off by yourself so late at night ... I was so worried that I immediately ... *atishoo!*'

'So embarrassing! Here, my shawl's a long one, wrap half of it around yourself. I can't give it to you entirely though, I can't afford to catch a cold myself.'

'Of course not, how can I use your shawl? Let's run on our way back instead—you won't be cold then.' Running back all the way to the IB, we discovered that the chowkidar had covered our cups of tea with lids and left. Near the head of the cot stood a lantern. He materialized again as we were drinking our tea.

'Your truck will leave at five in the morning. The driver's asked me to wake you up in time. Should I?'

'Of course you must. At four-thirty. And please make us a cup of tea too. All right?'

'*Zaroor*. Zaroor. Goodnight, Sir.' The chowkidar left with our cups.

'Go to bed, Lalwani. Goodnight.' I lay down.

'Goodnight.' Beanpole perched himself on the table, swinging his legs.

I lay down all right, but I wasn't comfortable.

'Aren't you going to sleep, Doctor?'

'In a minute.' The legs kept swinging. All sorts of shadows cast by the lantern trembled on the wall. Lengthening, shortening. The waterfall could be heard outside. The buzzing of wild insects. In the room, a sleepless young man.

Blast! He was making me very uncomfortable. I sat up. My eyes were drawn to the ceiling. And suddenly I saw ... what's that? A curtain wire ran across the ceiling to separate the room into two halves. Not a wire, but a rod. A heavy curtain hung along one wall. I hadn't realized in my excitement all this while that there was an arrangement to split the room into a drawing room and a dining room. Perfect. We could have separate waiting rooms for ladies and gents now. I had always been fond of games. You exist, god! You have ensured that Lalwani's chastity won't be harmed tonight. Glory to you!

Softly I called out to him, pointing with my finger.

'Doctor, there. Do you see those?'

'Curtains.'

'Oh yes, well done! Brilliant! Now draw the curtains and fall asleep, there's a good boy.

In a minute each of us had our own room, how fantastic.

I'd heard that this used to be the practice in Japan in older days. Paper curtains would be drawn to split rooms. They became walls.

Such innocent delight on the doctor's part on spotting the curtains. Leaping to the floor, he split the room into two in an instant, making himself invisible. But so what—he could still be seen knee downwards, all the way to his socks and shoes, beneath the curtain. Daddy Long Legs was probably laying out his bedding. Despite the drawn curtains all kinds of ghostly shadows danced on the wall. I turned the flame of the lantern on the floor even lower. The dance on the wall was reduced at once. Now for sleep.

'Good night, Doctor. Tuck yourself in now.' But when I looked in his direction, no, he wasn't in bed yet. There he was, perched on the table once more. Behind the purdah his boots were swinging madly. To hell with him. Let him do whatever he wanted.

How much does a man need?

There was no roof at first, a roof was found. A room too. There was no bed, a bed appeared. There was no privacy, and now there was privacy as well. And still he wasn't satisfied. What more did he want? Was he not going to be at peace till I left the room? But that wasn't going to happen. I was angry now.

'Doctor?'

'Yes, Madam?'

'Why don't you go to sleep?'

'...'

'Aren't you going to sleep?'

'...'

'Look here. I have no evil designs on you. What frightens you so? Tell me.'

'What? No, no, no ... what's all this, what on earth are you saying. Really. You are a *crazy* lady. Truly, dear god. The *things* you say. Oh....'

The doctor spoke fluently in his embarrassment. But he didn't go to bed.

All I said was 'Don't worry, Doctor, please relax. I promise you complete moral and physical safety....'

No response.

'Everything will be ok. Just relax, please. Try to sleep.... Doctor? Are you listening? Goodnight.'

[Kindly go to sleep, my boy, or else I'm the one who's going to start feeling afraid. He isn't mad, is he? My heart is infected with the fear of spending the night in the same room as a madman. Why is he so embarrassed? This isn't a bedroom for a newlywed couple, after all. My eyes are drooping with sleep. Que sera sera. Glory be. Good night, Daddy Long Legs.]

~

Wake Up, Miss Muffet

'Chai, Memsahib.'

I awoke to the chowkidar bellowing into my ear, tea in hand.

'Good morning, Memsahib.'

'Good morning, Chowkidar. Thank you.'

'The truck is ready.'

'Take this bedding away,' the doctor said suddenly from the other side. Daddy Long Legs was swinging his feet below the curtain. So strange! Hadn't he slept at all? How could he be up so early with his bedding all packed? Or hadn't he used it at all? Poor thing. Exclaiming 'Alas, my fearful pigeon', I should be 'enfolding him in my bosom' this instant, like Mohan the Bandit from the popular series. After all, that was how he regarded me. My presence had led him into the Chapter of Death. Mind you, I was quite thrilled. Who'd have thought that the mere existence of an innocent creature like me could prove quite so sinister to someone? My greatest regret is that all my friends feel utterly secure entrusting their husbands to me, that's how much of a vegetarian I am. No one harbours even the faintest suspicion.

Still, suppressing with great effort the desire to belt out *'Hum tum ... ek kamre mein bandh ho, our chabi kho jaay,'* I said, 'Good morning, Doctor. Did you sleep well?'

'Yes, thank you.'

'Want some tea?'

'Yes, thank you.'

By the time I returned from the bathroom the doctor was ready, dressed in a green sweater, his hair slicked back with Brylcreem. It was he who signed the IB register as we drank our tea, which gave me no chance. For one thing, the room wasn't strictly speaking a 'room', and for another, it wasn't permitted to allow two people to share one room. The government wouldn't realize that the chowkidar had only rescued two hapless humans. The register said the name of the place was Jamiri. Only now had I found out.

'Just two and a half rupees?' I was astonished.

'Only because you're alone,' the chowkidar informed me ruefully.

'It would have been one and a half if you'd been married. Unmarried people are charged more.' It was his turn to be astonished as I handed him two rupees when leaving. His sudden delighted smile made it obvious that Jamiri was not accustomed to tourists. It was mainly government officers and contractors who travelled on this route, and they didn't need to offer tips. The chowkidars in these regions were different from their counterparts in other tourist dak bungalows.

Jamiri was wondrously beautiful during a half-bloomed dawn. The river flowed swiftly in the ravine below, the colours of autumn were visible on trees all around, and so many waterfalls! The hills were full of these little torrents, just like the ones I had seen on the road to Darjeeling as a child, when we lost count because there were so many.

Sometimes we passed hilly villages, where all the children had such sweet faces. And the cats were all grey and plump.

Manchand was showing no signs of having had a few drinks the night before. The incense sticks were burning again.

Everyone was looking alert. Myla and Manchand smiled sweetly to signal good morning. Mr Sen wasn't tipsy at all. With a smile he said, 'Good morning, Mrs Sen, good morning Doctor Sahib.'

Nothing compares to mornings in the mountains. It was quite cold. A shawl wasn't enough, so I had also put on a sleeveless sweater. The most beautiful sights surrounded us. I had never seen such a pretty jungle road anywhere else in India's mountain regions. Enormous vines wound their way upwards around the tall trees, and it was impossible to count the varieties of flowers that had bloomed in October. The Kameng River raced along next to us. Why is that there is always a river alongside virtually any mountain road? When I had made this astonishingly original observation to Amartya as a grown-up student, while driving along the Colorado River in the Rocky Mountains, he hadn't known how to hide his embarrassment at my ignorance. 'You mean you didn't know that it's rivers that cut ravines into mountains? That's why we build our roads in the spaces created by rivers. It's the roads that run alongside rivers, not the other way round.'

I had become wiser since then, but hadn't corrected the mistaken perspective of my childhood. There was that turbulent milk-white river which had pranced along as it raced the train in which I was travelling as a child with my parents to Interlaken in the Alps. I had been convinced ever since then that it's rivers which run alongside roads. Since I couldn't see the road itself, I assumed it was the primary object. This entire valley was called the Kameng Valley. The Kameng was the life spring of this area. It was the Kameng that bore me all the way to Tawang.

From Jamiri to Dedja. A small place. We got off at a village in the hills for a cup of tea. From there to Tenga, which was slightly larger, where we had breakfast. Tea and toast. The rest of them had eggs as well. The road kept getting prettier, as did the mountain. And I no longer needed a helping hand from anyone to lower myself backwards from the truck to the ground. I still needed a little help to climb back in, though. I was clearly gaining in expertise in this new form of truck travel.

Mr Sen asked over breakfast at Tenga, 'Where will you stay at Bomdila? Doctors can always find a place in a hospital or medical centre. They're part of the Kameng Medical Service. But where will *you* stay for three days?'

'Three days? What do you mean?'

'Oh, we're going to halt at Bomdila for three days before leaving for Tawang. We have some work here till the first of next month.'

'Really? The doctor's going to stay at Bomdila too?'

'How should I know? Don't you know what his plan is? What's yours, for that matter?'

I am in great awe of the word 'plan'. I respect it deeply. But alas, you could say it has no place in my life.

'My plan? What do you suppose? Get to Tawang as quickly as possible. I have no wish to halt at Bomdila. What's the point? And where will I stay?'

'If that's a problem I can make arrangements. There are many Bengali families in Bomdila. There are bungalows too. Probably hotels as well.'

'No need, I'll just go on to Tawang.'

'But how? We're not going.'

'Oh ... no!'

'That's what I'm saying.'

'Doctor?'

'Yes, Madam?'

'They're going to stop in Bomdila for three days. Did you know?'

'Is that so? That makes things difficult. I had no idea. I was told the truck's going to Tawang.'

'What are you going to do, then?'

'Let's see. I'll have to take another truck. I'm sure there will be one at Bomdila. Or a jeep. I can take the local bus too. I'll manage.'

'But listen, Doctor. I'm coming with you too.' The doctor did not reply.

As soon as the words escaped my lips, I realized I'd made a mistake. The doctor would be terrified now. I'd blundered.

'I'm twenty years senior to you, Doctor. Old enough to be your father. Don't be afraid without reason....' [There's me and my wife, and those nine sons of ours....]

'Only twenty? Not two hundred?'

The doctor dropped a bombshell.

What was he thinking?

Looking at him closely, I detected traces of a smile.

He didn't seem to be annoyed. Now he was speaking again.

'You can't be older than my eldest sister. My father is seventy-two.'

'Same thing. Six of one.... The thing is, I'm not twenty-six like you. Don't be *too* shy, or we'll both find the going difficult.'

'Not to worry, Mrs Sen. We'll find our way to Tawang.'

At Bomdila we got out of Manchand's truck. Mr Sen was in charge of the rations it was carrying. His job was to distribute the material to different shops and maintain the accounts. I asked Manchand 'How much should I pay?' 'Pay?' Myla laughed. So did Manchand. 'Nothing. This isn't a bus or a train,' said Mr Sen. 'We gave you a lift. The company is paying for the trip. If you want to give a tip, give it to the driver and cleaner. That's up to you.'

The doctor gave twenty rupees.

I did too.

Both Manchand and Myla were delighted.

'Goodbye, Manchand, we'll meet again. Thank you, Myla. Bye bye. We'll be on our way, Mr Sen. Lovely meeting you.'

'Lovely meeting you too. Over there, that's where all the trucks stop. You're bound to get a lift to Tawang.'

~

Fikar Not

Indeed we did.

It was another ration truck. But it wasn't stuffed, being loaded with only a few sacks filled with goods. The driver was a young Nepali named Ghanashyam Chhetri. There were two other young men with him, but not in the cab, because they preferred riding in the back of the truck, under the sky. Only the doctor and I sat up front with the driver, who was a happy-go-lucky sort, not solemn like Manchand. My impression was that truck drivers were all drunks who drove at reckless speeds. But Manchand had said that the tradition of driving in the hills was different. They didn't even touch alcohol when at the wheel, for this would invite the curse of the goddess.

'Do you drink?' I asked Ghanashyam.

'Of course, Madam,' he said, scratching his head diffidently.

'Have you had a drink now?'

He bit his tongue in dismay.

'Never by daylight, Memsahib. Only when we halt for the night. It's a sin for a driver to drink when on duty.'

So, whether they're Jats or Nepalis, the dharma of driving in the hills is the same. If you touch alcohol, you cannot touch the steering.

But then consider the road.

One hairpin bend after another.

The mountain road kept curving as tightly as the top of a hairpin. And the entire route was plastered with notices, all of which seemed to be for army drivers. Who knows, perhaps they were not indoctrinated in the faith of civilian drivers. Most of them began with the words *Fikar not*, followed by all kinds of homilies. *Better late than never! Someone is waiting for you!* The one closest to my heart was this one: *What's the hurry to pass from the hills to heaven?* There were many more pearls of wisdom. *Look for a tiger at every turn.* Or, *Accident to you, misery to others! Smile and drive, live and let live! Be soft on my curves!* We kept passing army camps along the way. Here, the notices said: *Thairo! MP ko report karo!* At last I realized what this creature named Hindi in Roman letters was. So *Fikar not* meant *Not to worry* in Hinglish (or Eindi?).

We stopped at Dirang village for a cup of tea. A gigantic camp named Dirangjang had been set up next to the wide and fast-flowing Dirang River. The truck continued along the ribbon of a road winding upwards. The camps included small cinema halls with tin roofs like warehouses. I noticed several halls with the same name on the way. 'Ball of Fire'. What films were they running? Hindi movies, whose posters were stuck on the walls.

A stream of armoured vehicles trundled along the road. Only one or two flimsy, ramshackle buses were visible. Trucks like ours, however, were many. But it was essentially the army that used this road. A parade of Shaktiman trucks manufactured by Tata-Mercedes passed us every now and then, the vehicles filled with young men. They appeared to be north Indian—Sikh soldiers were the most prominent. Maybe Sikhs were just more visible than others.

We stopped for lunch at Rama Camp. My first source of excitement here was a small furry creature similar to a buffalo.

What on earth was this animal? The penny dropped when I got a glimpse of the tail, I knew him, gentle reader, I knew him. The creature with the bushy tail was none other than a yak. Ecstatic to have spotted my first female yak, I entered the hotel for lunch. Excellent rice and meat, washed down with hot tea. Plump, hairy, happy Bhutia dogs roamed around everywhere. The more I saw them, the more I wanted to pick them up and take them home. After the meal I rinsed my hands in a waterfall behind the hotel. Lovely cold water. How smoothly it flowed over the mossy rocks. So many ferns growing on the banks. I wish I could express how refreshed I felt after dipping my hands in the water and sprinkling it on my face.

An exquisite scene presented itself on the mountain slopes near Ahirgarh. What they called 'fall' or 'autumn colours' in North America—a flame of colours lit up the jungles over there before the leaves began to drop. Some of the leaves changed colour—yellow-to-saffron-to-orange-to-brown, vermilion red, blood red, powdery red—like the maple or the oak. Some were evergreen, while the explosion of colours on the rest were visible in the tranquil gaps. It was all strangely intoxicating. Going out in groups on weekends to take in the beauty of fall colours was an annual American pastime.

From where had I arrived in the midst of this 'impetuous winter-daring autumn' of Jibanananda Das? Would I ever have known of the autumnal magic that exists in my own country had I not visited these mountains of the east?

The terrain grew increasingly mountainous, the forests increasingly sparse, the air increasingly cold. The waterfalls were still plentiful. We stopped for afternoon tea at a place named Sangezu. Two impossibly beautiful young women served us, and began to chat up Ghanashyam. They were dressed in

Tibetan *baku*s with white blouses and aprons round their waists. They even had a small stationery shop here, where they sold, along with daily necessities, very pretty and warm Tibetan jackets at just fifty rupees each. Stuffed jackets of Chinese silk with brocade and wool embroidery. Of regal appearance, and very, very warm. There were bakus and aprons on sale too. I'd buy some on the way back. But the tea here was wonderful.

Daylight was waning. One more village appeared by the side of the road. Every village had its name on a signboard. There was a landslide in my heart when I read this one.

Shangri-La.

Wasn't Shangri-La the miraculous village in Tibet? The land of eternal youth tucked away in one corner of the snowy world of the Himalayas, which time had forgotten to touch. The magical village in *The Lost Horizon*. Was that how far we'd travelled?

And then I saw another gigantic signboard hung up on the hillside. It read, *The Lost Horizon*, accompanied by a long notice in the English language. But our truck drove past so quickly that despite straining my eyes I could not read it in that autumn twilight. All I could make out was the words *Closed from December to April*. But neither the doctor nor Ghanashyam had any idea what exactly was closed. Nor did they know that the people of Shangri-La were invincible and immortal. How could they be so ignorant, despite living in such proximity? Neither of them had watched the film *The Lost Horizon* or even heard of it. Although Ghanashyam did watch 'Angrezi pictures' from time to time.

It took just that one name, Shangri-La, to make me feel in my blood that I had indeed travelled a long way, to a land of fantasy much farther, much more unknown, than London or New York, under the mysterious shadow of the veil of Tibet.

But what that brief glimpse gave me a view of was not women of eternal life who had left their senescence behind, but Sikh soldiers.

Shangri-La was now an enormous army camp!

The pinewoods were beginning to look denuded now. It was getting colder. The road ran steeply uphill. The next village was named Baisakhi. A tiny village 11,500 feet above sea level. The road grew steeper. Soon we arrived at Tse-La. This pass is at a height of 14,000 feet. It is apparently the second-highest motorable road in the world, with the highest (also in the Himalaya), on the western side, the Lahaul-Spiti Road in Ladakh. (The Karakoram Highway had not opened yet. I don't know if the pecking order remains unchanged or whether Karakoram has defeated the others.)

There was a stone memorial at Tse-La that read, *This road from SELA (13,714) to Tawang dedicated by Mrs Ruth Marley on 14 December 1972 to commemorate the work done by these units of 14 Border Roads Task Force, Fikar Not Fourteen, & to remember the men of the force who died with snow boots on.*

At last I realized the full significance of 'Fikar Not'. Those who had braved the cold and the snow month after month, cutting through mountains and forests to build this road, were the Fikar Not team. Indeed, who else could the genuine Fikar Not people possibly be?

Apparently there was a *gompa* close by, the Tse-La Gompa. The enshrined goddess was known to be extremely receptive. There were old Tibetan manuscripts too, Ghanashyam informed us. But we couldn't go, since the road was not motorable, and there was no time to walk. So visiting the gompa was out of the question.

Tse-La was perpetually shrouded in mist. A couple of other trucks had also halted. There were no tea shops here, though.

Why were people getting off, then? Ah, the call of nature was being addressed behind the curtain of mist, on the other side of the rocks. The trees provided no screens here.

Seeing the doctor and Ghanashyam walking into the distance rather philosophically, I set off in the opposite direction. Any spot that seemed to offer some privacy also seemed to have been discovered by someone else already.

There was a thin layer of frost on the ground. The mountain road was draped in grey autumn dusk. I spotted several billy goats surveying me, holding their horns aloft while their ears twitched. They were being herded by a young boy. Where had they come from? There didn't seem to be a village nearby. They must have walked a long way. With evening falling, it was time they returned. I too made my way back to the lorry.

The road began to descend after this—going down all the way to a picturesque lake. The place was covered in frost. I seemed to remember seeing just such a lake from the plane while flying over Pamir. The ice and water were an extraordinary green. I did not know what Mansarovar was like. This one was completely covered in ice. A row of snow-covered peaks in the distance was suddenly bathed in orange and purple by the setting sun. The lake lay in the lap of the mountain. I spotted a sledge being drawn along by four powerful, furry dogs. A child sat in it, holding a basket. The boy was wrapped from head to toe, like an Eskimo. For an instant the entire scene was transformed into the polar region. The ice-covered lake stretching to the horizon, the rows of white mountain peaks standing over then, the child in the sledge in the foreground—all of it seemed to be so much out of a geography book that my own existence felt unreal there.

'Yashwantgarh is named after the soldier Yashwant Singh,' said Ghanashyam Chhetri. 'A Sikh soldier named Yashwant

Singh was manning this post single-handedly in the 1962 war. He kept firing, providing cover to his comrades as they retreated, giving the Chinese troops the impression that a large battalion was still stationed here. All of them except Yashwant had withdrawn. He had chosen to play this role to save the others. All of them would have died otherwise. Eventually the Chinese did show up and kill him. The place has been called Yashwantgarh since then.

'Tell the rest of the story too,' said the doctor.

'The rest?' Ghanashyam smiled.

'The soldiers claim Yashwant has not left his post yet. No one dares fall asleep here on sentry duty. The moment they do, a resounding slap lands on their face. Yashwant Singh spares no one who sleeps on duty....'

'I hope Yashwant Singh doesn't create trouble unless provoked. He won't shove us off the road as we pass, will he?'

The doctor protested loudly. 'Of course not, he is a benevolent spirit....'

'I see.'

'The Tibetans are great believers in spirits. They refer to ghosts as *jung*s. They have many different tribes of ghosts and spirits. All inhabitants of the mountains seem to believe in ghosts. So does the military. Perhaps it's natural for those for whom accidental death is a constant companion to believe in spirits and dissatisfied souls.'

~

Of Man and Trout

There was a trout farm at Nuruanang. One of the branches of the Kameng River had been dammed, and trout were farmed in the reservoir. Like the koi carp, trout also try to swim against the current. They can leap a long way out of the water too.

At a trout farm in Oxford I'd seen currents and waves being generated artificially in a tank, and the trout constantly leaping out of the water (it's good for their health), two of them falling to the hard dry cement floor outside. They were instantly picked up in nets attached to the end of bamboo poles and deposited back in the water. The same nets were used to scoop them out to be sold.

My father-in-law used to go trout-fishing in Kullu–Manali. The mountain springs there are full of the fish. The Kameng trout farm was a huge government enterprise. I was told that there were farms like these in Kashmir too. The truck halted at Nuruanang. Meanwhile, one more passenger had joined us at the back. Who knew where he had climbed on? One of the two young men who had been there from the start was the cleaner of the truck. The other one's clothes showed signs of affluence. He didn't exactly seem a villager. Nor a contractor type. All of us got off the truck at Nuruanang. We would have a cup of tea here.

I learnt from the young man that he was a student in Tezpur. His parents lived in a village near Tawang. Something happened as we were walking.

We suddenly found a fish lying on the rocky trail we were walking on. Was it dead or alive? The student stopped to pick it up. It was medium-sized, at least 400 or 500 grams in weight. As soon as he grabbed the fish, it sprayed a white liquid on his brand-new sweater. At once a mask seemed to descend on the pleasant appearance of this young man from the mountains. Kneeling, he hammered the fish on the head with a stone until it was dead.

I felt miserable.

A primal desire for revenge seemed to be associated with his behaviour. How horrible the word 'vengeance' is, isn't it? This was the face of vengeance. A helpless creature had tried to defend itself in the course of nature, and a powerful creature had avenged this attack, also in the course of nature. It wasn't as though we didn't catch fish, or slaughter goats or chicken. But there was an uncontrolled aspect to this act, with no difference between fish and man.

At this moment a security guard appeared and—I couldn't believe my eyes—arrested the young man. On charges of murdering the fish. Catching and killing fish in the region of a trout farm was a punishable offence. The young man kept begging pardon, with quite some aggression thrown in, and eventually the sentry released him without taking a bribe or anything.

~

Nuruanang Inn

A small tea shop stood next to a mountain stream cascading over terraces, and ending in a dam. It was more or less a shanty—a hill edition of the roadside dhaba. It was dark inside. A group was seated in the first room, drinking tea and eating out of bowls. The food was also being cooked in the same place. There was an even smaller room next to this one, with a fire blazing in a tin in the middle. This was the fireplace, called the *bukhari* here. Kashmir had its kangri, smaller versions of which people clutched to their chests beneath their shawls. But the bukhari wasn't used the same way. The room was filled with wood smoke. It was quite warm from the fire. Several stools were arranged around the bukhari, with a bench and table on one side. We began with two bowls of tea each, followed by a bowl of *thukpa*. How horrible this thukpa tasted! No salt, no chillies, no oil, no ghee, no meat, no vegetables—heaven knew what it actually contained. Apparently it consisted of a few pieces of dried yak meat and some cheap army surplus meat. It was as bland as starch, but still we gobbled it down because we were starving. Besides, it had suddenly turned much colder. The journey of the hot thukpa down the throat into the stomach was quite pleasant. After the thukpa, another bowl of tea, which arrived in porcelain bowls instead of cups or glasses. There was so much smoke in the room that we couldn't see one another's faces. I was severely allergic to wood smoke—in Calcutta or Santiniketan or Delhi, I would have collapsed by now. But whenever I was on the road I carried with me the god of travellers, who protected me at every step. The bill for six cups of tea and two bowls of thukpa came to three rupees in all. The doctor footed it entirely, without letting me pay my share.

There were no bright lights in the poky smoke-filled little room. The flames from the bukhari dispelled as much of the gloom as they could. Several figures wrapped in blankets were sitting there, sunk in darkness.

'They're drinking *chhang*.'

'And what might chhang be?'

'It's like beer.'

'I see.'

'They're drinking *raksi* too.'

'What's that?'

'A stronger liquor.'

'Let's go, let's go,' Ghanashyam Chhetri began to hurry us. 'We won't get there before ten. Have to stop at Jang. Some things have to be delivered.' The doctor said he had to stop at Jang too. We left Nuruanang Inn.

The last army camp was at the eastern edge of Jang. There were no other army stations beyond this point. Neither India's nor China's. A total of forty miles (or was it kilometres? who knew?) of military-free terrain. Jeep-babu had said bunkers were being constructed underground, and that they were teeming with Indians on one side and Chinese on the other. But alas, no one would give me the address, which meant I would never see this sight with my own eyes.

At Jang the truck went off on its own devices, while the doctor made me get off with him after fixing a rendezvous with Chhetri.

The person whose house I visited in the military barracks with the doctor was a Kashmiri named Colonel Devdutt. His beautiful wife and two angelic children lived with him. This meant that the army must have had its own school there too. Colonel Devdutt's wife and children were delighted to see me. They immediately concluded that the doctor was there with his wife. It was obvious they didn't have too many women guests hereabouts.

It was quite late, ten at night. The children had gone to bed, but they jumped out on seeing us. Mrs Devdutt gave us gulab jamuns. She wanted to offer us coffee too, but there was no time. The doctor had bought some brandy and tins of condensed milk at the army disposals canteen, which was handed over. With the conversations delaying us, the truck was heard blowing its horn outside. We ran.

The doctor was holding a carton with his shopping in both his hands. Neither of us had a torch. It was a long mountain trail. We were taking a different route back—the meeting spot was elsewhere. The path was unfamiliar. I was running blindly behind the doctor in the darkness. Only after getting into the truck did I remember the torch in my bag. The trail was rocky, but, how fortunate, not covered with ice like Nuruanang or Tse-La. My foot struck something as we were running. I picked it up. A small fruit like a pomegranate. I had indeed noticed children eating ripe pomegranates, even crunching raw peaches like guavas, and indolent old men squatting by the road slicing giant cucumbers as large as gourds with the knives tucked into their waistbands. As I ran with the small fruit in my hand, a long beam of light fell on the road in front of me. The driver had lit his headlights to make it easier for us. It was simple now, and soon we were sitting in the truck, panting.

Rolling his eyes at the carton, the driver said, 'Rum?'

'Brandy.'

'Same thing.'

~

Caught in the Heartless Beams

Suddenly the smoothness of the journey was broken, causing anxiety rather than excitement. Two small animals were
trapped in the circle of the headlights—a pair of stubby
mountain ponies. They had been ambling along in the secure
and secluded darkness of the mountains when cruel arrows of
light suddenly began to chase them. Although they galloped
as fast as they could, the ponies could not escape the racing
truck's headlights. Over and over I asked Ghanashyam to turn
them off, but he said that was impossible. He kept dipping
and dimming the lights alternately, but that confused the
ponies further, who began to gallop erratically now. Not once
did it occur to me to say 'Slow down, let them run away from
the beams'. That solution came to mind much later. By then
the ponies were about to be run over after their exhausting
run against the truck. I was terrified that they might miss
their footing or become so frightened that they would fall into
the ravine. In distress I clasped them to my heart, fearing for
their lives, until the road widened and Ghanashyam Chhetri's
demonic truck could race past them. I had never been on a
hunt, but I realized how the quarry might feel when chased
by the hunter. The foolish ponies had no idea that they were
not being chased to be killed. To them all men were probably predators and huntsmen—all animals must be afraid of
humans, the only living beings who kill members of their own

species. Animals battle one another too, causing injuries, but only with the intention to defeat, not to kill. Human beings are the only creatures who kill other humans even after they have admitted defeat. Animals let the vanquished go.

~

Andhe Kinare Andhi Raate, Jaayen toh Jaayen Kahan

Asking the driver to stop the truck, the doctor said, 'I'm getting off here. This is where I live.' Jumping down, he went to the back of the truck to get his bedding out.

'Where will *you* get off?' When Chhetri posed this question, it occurred to me for the first time that I had nowhere to spend the night in Tawang.

'Me? No IB here?'

'There's a Circuit House, but it's closed now. There's no one there. Have you got a letter?'

'No. I don't have a letter or anything like that.'

Suddenly I saw the doctor, his luggage unloaded, holding his hand out tentatively.

'Goodbye, Dr Sen.'

'Wait, just a minute, Doctor. Is there any way to get the Circuit House unlocked?'

'At this hour? It's past ten-thirty after all—there isn't even any power here now; everyone's gone to bed at nine.'

'Besides, the ADC is in Bomdila,' said Chhetri. 'I met him there. She doesn't even have a letter; no one will unlock the Circuit House for her.'

'Where do I go then? Is there a hotel or something?'

'Here? A hotel here?' The truck driver chuckled. 'You made no arrangements before coming here? Whom are you visiting? Where do you want to go?'

Oh my, Ghanashyam Chhetri.

'I'm here for the gompa. I want to go to the gompa.'

'But that's tomorrow morning. What about tonight?'

'I'd better go,' the doctor said hastily. 'It's late.'

'What do mean? Where do you think you're going without me? I'm coming too....'

'Where?'

'To your house, obviously.'

'Oh no, that's impossible, I'm a bachelor.'

'So? Do you live beneath a tree because you're a bachelor? Don't you have a house?'

'I do, but there's no one else there.'

'Just as well, there'll be enough room.'

'But, that's impossible ... I live alone ... my house ...'

'Do you have just the one room?' asked the driver.

'Four rooms. Official quarters.'

'Then what's the problem? Take Madam with you. Else we'll have to take her to our home. How can she live in our slum? It'll be too hard for her.'

'I'd have gone with you even if you had just one room, Shyam, my friend. It's a proven fact that I'm a chaste woman. What are you afraid of?'

'I'm wondering what Bahadur will think.'

'Who's Bahadur?'

'He looks after the house.'

'You're not alone in that case. Then there's nothing to fear. Bahadur will protect you. Come on now, take my suitcase, let me get off the truck.'

A figure loomed up in the darkness to take the doctor's luggage and bedding and started walking. The doctor took my suitcase with great reluctance. I didn't see how much he paid Chhetri, but I gave him twenty rupees. He had fed me with a constant supply of paan during the journey. He had even taken some photographs out of his pocket to show me. I had no idea what they were photographs of. Chhetri said, 'These are pictures of the hydroelectric project at Tawang. I took them with my own camera.' Not that there was the slightest sign of water in any of the photographs. They could easily be pictures of the tiger project in the Sunderbans, or of a drought project in Bankura District. Still, he had been pleasant company. He refused the money at first, but then pocketed it. I held out my hand to shake his and say goodbye—he was delighted.

Then I followed the doctor. The road was so narrow we had to walk single file. Remembering my torch, I took it out and turned it on. It couldn't exactly be called a road, it was just a shortcut carved out of the hillside. Leaping over a wall with his long legs, the doctor made his way inside his house. And got into trouble at once. With me.

'The gate is on the other side. This is the back of my house. Wait there. I'll come round the front, we'll have to walk a long way.'

'What for? You think I can't jump over a wall? It's not much of one anyway.' Balancing myself on one hand, I vaulted over the wall.

'Good!' There seemed to be laughter in his voice. The doctor had finally deigned to smile. How strange! Did he have no sense at all? He should have realized long ago that jumping over such a low earthen wall would be child's play for me. Wasn't I the one who had erected an invisible wall inside the room at the Jamiri bungalow?

When we got inside it turned out to be quite a nice house. Bahadur made me sit down in an enormous room furnished with only a lantern and two wooden high-backed chairs with armrests. And an icy atmosphere.

The doctor asked me, 'Some tea?'

'Of course.'

'Some milk and rice?'

'If you have some.'

'He'll make it.'

'I'd like to have a bath. Can't shake off the tiredness of two days of travel without one.'

'Then get ready quickly, the water's being heated. But don't pour water over your head at night, just the body. And put on your overcoat immediately afterwards, or you'll catch a cold. It's a sly chill out here.'

I was telling myself that I have been in much colder places, my friend, minus thirty, where I wouldn't have felt anything even if Tamburlaine were to slice off the end of my nose with his sword.

But then that was outdoors.

Indoors it was the claustrophobic comfort of the central heating system. In America there was no fear of catching a cold after a bath, but it was a distinct possibility during my first stay in England. On getting out of the hot water tub after your bath, you had to shiver in the ice-cold bathroom as you dried yourself, put on your clothes, and then quickly get under the blanket with a hot-water bottle in your ice-cold bedroom. This bottle was not a bottle, but a bag. Gradually England acquired heating pads and electric blankets, and central heating is quite prevalent now. Bedrooms seldom had heaters or a fireplace. Everyone used to say then that it was healthy to have cold bedrooms. Perhaps it was a foolproof method to prevent asphyxiation. As a student in Trinity College, Amartya had to sleep in one building and bathe in another, with a giant yard separating the two. The perfect arrangement to make sure you caught a cold on a winter night. As a result the young men cut down their weekly baths to fortnightly, monthly, and even tri-monthly ones. As winter intensified, bath days diminished.

But all this was twenty-five years ago. *O tempora, o mores.* Trinity must have central heating by now, attached showers too. Perhaps the young men bathe every night before going to bed. The times they are a-changin'.

No sooner had I finished my tea than Bahadur said the hot water was ready. The bathroom was right next door. It had two cold water taps and a shower. Not even the fireplaces in Calcutta's Westernized mansions could be more redundant and meaningless than that shower. Steam was rising from a canister placed beneath the taps, with my bathwater in it. I turned on the cold water tap for a trickle to cool the steaming water and went into the room to fetch my clothes and towel and soap. It didn't even take a minute, but by the time I was back, the water was ice-cold. An icicle was clinging to the tap. No, I hadn't experienced this in either the UK or the US. Bahadur brought me some hot water again a little later, pouring hot water over the tap to reinstate the flow of water. I did feel refreshed after a bath. The doctor's bedroom was quite warm. I ran into it. There was a bukhari in the centre of the room, its chimney rising through the ceiling. Its presence had split the room. On one side were a small desk, chair, and a bookrack. There was a mirror on the wall, a comb and shaving things on a shelf, along with Brylcreem and powder. On the other side was a narrow bed. It was a single man's room—how many things could he possibly need? I was surprised when I rummaged through his bookrack. It should have held James

Hadley Chase and Harold Robbins, but oh no, this one had the Bhagavad Gita and the Upanishad. And, *thank god*, a few Agatha Christies.

The doctor had gone out. I didn't know where he had gone at that hour of the night with his torch. He came back with a huge mattress under his arm.

'I borrowed this from a friend.'

'For me?'

'No, for me. You're sleeping in my bed.'

Bahadur brought some milk and rice. As I was getting ready for bed, the doctor said, 'Have a bit of brandy. It'll help in this cold.' Not a bad idea. Whether it helped in the cold or not, it would definitely help the body. Who knew how tomorrow would go? After the baby milk, some smooth brandy silk.

~

One, Two, Three, Four, There's the Bed, There's the Door

I had gulped down my two spoonfuls of brandy. The doctor was sipping his. But he wasn't talking. With nothing else to do, I went to bed.

'Where will you sleep?'

'In the other room.'

'Has the bed been made?'

'Bahadur will do it.'

'Won't you be cold?'

'No.'

'Do you have a bukhari there?'

'No.'

'A bed?'

'No.'

'A carpet.'

'There aren't even curtains, never mind a carpet.'

'Sounds like a fantastic room. You can't sleep there, my friend. You'd better sleep in your own room. I'll move into the other one. I'd have had to spend the night on the road, this is a thousand times better. I'll sleep there.'

'Of course not. This is your room. There's a bukhari, there's a bed. You cannot sleep in the other room, I'll go.'

I got out of bed. Next door I found a narrow bed made up on the floor of a huge, empty room. The air was ice-cold, making you shiver as soon as you entered. Bahadur had gone to sleep outside the room, in the corridor. A lantern hung near the door.

Oh dear, this was bound to lead to pneumonia. Was this where Mr Doctor was going to 'bravely go to sleep at night'? Or this Ms, for that matter? Were we mad?

I said, 'Bahadur, please take the doctor's bedding into his own bedroom. And you must sleep there too. It's freezing here.'

Bahadur laid out the bedding on the floor of the bedroom. The doctor objected vigorously, but did not stop him. This was the only warm space. The other one really was far too cold. Even the corridor was less icy, being a closed space, after all. The window pane was broken in the other room, making it even colder.

The first problem now was, what to wear to bed? Without getting into a discussion, both of us went to bed dressed in outdoor clothes. The only things we took off were our shoes.

The next problem was the door. Bolt it or leave it unbolted? The heat would escape if it wasn't closed.

But if we did close it, what would Bahadur...? So the doctor wanted to leave it unbolted. But we bolted it eventually. Bahadur was asked to sleep just outside the door, only because there was no room for him inside. Since Bahadur was perpetually expressionless, it was impossible to surmise what he was thinking. Nor was it clear why, in this distant land where the doctor had no one of his own, he was treating Bahadur with the deference due an elderly uncle. All this reluctance and anxiety should have been mine, since I was the one born a female.

These were like a natural skin for women, not only biologically, by virtue of nature, but also sociologically, as a result of the rules imposed by society. But I felt none of these, while this young man, this six-foot-tall Sindhi doctor, was chafing, all knotted up in the ropes and chains of all these constraints. Poor fellow. How could someone with such blue eyes, who looked exactly like Amitabh Bachchan from a distance, be this way?

I was now inordinately tempted to tease the boy. Should I charge at him romantically, singing 'Tonight I will play holy with you, Shyam, you are alone in the woods and here I am'? What would the doctor do then? Would he immolate himself to avoid being defiled? Would he whip out a kukri and commit murder? Had he already spent one sleepless night in the light and dark of desire and anxiety in Jamiri? The male character was beyond Devsen's ken. Don't overthink it. 'Sleep well, Doctor, it's very kind of you to offer me a shelter. Good night, Doctor.'

And so I fell asleep snugly. The doctor too must have slept comfortably on his bed on the floor. Given the warmth and safety of his own room, with the ever-alert Bahadur on guard at the door, he had no reason to stay awake. Never mind that there was a woman as formidable as a rogue elephant in the room.

~

First Day, First Light

Up at dawn, with the doctor still asleep on the floor. On opening the door, no Bahadur outside. The front door unlocked. And a breathtaking sight as soon as I stepped outside.

It was five-thirty by the clock, and the sun was about to rise. We were surrounded by mountains on all sides—and behind those mountains were the rays of the sun, just the way we used to draw them as children. The beams had scattered on the distant snow peaks. There weren't any trees to be seen, it was silent everywhere. An unbelievable tranquillity prevailed. The picture of dawn, without the sounds of dawn. Not a single bird could be heard.

There was a dilapidated Tibetan temple right behind the house. A gompa. The sun seemed to have chosen its spot, rising just behind it. It was like a theatre set. Naturally. It was the same sun that had stylishly set exactly between two curved coconut trees that time I was visiting Kanyakumari with Raj and Sarasamma—just like those clichéd calendar photographs. Here too it had created a dramatic moment for itself. This geriatric sun had no match when it came to grabbing attention. Who else had his experience? There was just another one who did—the moon.

This immense silence, with not a bird crying, made my skin prickle. Putting on my coat, I set out towards the gompa. This was not the Tawang gompa, which was an elaborate affair—like a fort, with a temple inside. Ghanashyam Chhetri had told me all this in the truck yesterday. Pointing to a village on the way, he had said 'There was a fort here. The Khampas unleashed a reign of terror on the Mompas and extracted steep taxes. They would lock their prisoners underground. The Khampas were from Tibet. Eventually the Mompas beat them back and threw them out so that they could live in peace.' I assumed this must have been after the advent of the British. It was Chhetri who had said, 'There's a fort at the Tawang Gompa too—outside. There's a lot of gold in the gompa; if it hadn't been for the fort, the Khampa robbers would have looted everything.'

But surely there was no gold in this gompa. It was a small temple, a tiny two-storeyed stone building. There was no question of a fort or anything here. About to enter, I found some sort of grain scattered on the veranda in front, set out to dry. They looked like seeds of grass. Four shaggy dogs, comfortably ensconced amidst them, began to bark at the top of their voices on seeing me, shattering the calm silence of the winter morning.

I'm not afraid of dogs. I love them, in fact. As soon as I went up to them, trying to pacify them by whistling, oh my god! Their barks grew louder. All these ascetic dogs from gompas were in a class of their own. Giving up my attempts to enter, I decided to walk around the temple instead. They fell silent at once. There was a prayer wheel outside. Spinning it amounted to chanting 'Om Mani Padme Hum' a hundred and eight times. A narrow stone staircase wound its way up outside the building to the first floor. A lama in saffron robes came down the stairs.

'Namaskar.'

'…' He returned my greeting.

'May I come into the gompa?' (In Hindi.)

'…' He took me along, but I couldn't make out anything of what he was saying. The dogs were ecstatic to see him, wagging their stumpy tails and following him into the temple. I had never seen dogs enter a temple before. I can't say I didn't feel uncomfortable. But I followed them in.

There was quite a large hall inside, with the prayer platform at one end. There was a pedestal there, which should have had a statue of the Buddha. But where was it? Have some faith, reader. Who was that enshrined in great reverence on the platform, in front of the sacred lamp? A plaster-of-Paris statue of Jawaharlal Nehru, complete with his waistcoat and Gandhi cap. Incense sticks were burning in front of this figure, while photographs of Indira Gandhi and Sanjay Gandhi were hung everywhere. There were large posters with quotations from Sanjay's speeches. What I enjoyed the most were the *thanka* paintings. I had seen Tibetan thankas earlier. Tibetan gods and goddesses painted in earth colours on silk, with zari and satin brocade above and below, and wooden strips attached like frames on top and bottom, with tassels underneath.

Here, too, there were many such thankas, except that instead of the Tibetan pantheon, there were individual as well as group photographs of Jawaharlal Nehru, Indira Gandhi, and Sanjay Gandhi. Sometimes all by themselves, sometimes in a crowd. An abundance of photographs of them delivering speeches from daises.

This place was so far and so high—had the news of Indira Gandhi and Sanjay Gandhi's ouster not arrived yet? It was November of 1977—the Sanjay comet had fallen from the sky as far back as in March. There were, however, a handful of morose, unreverenced, neglected figures of Buddha, caked with dust, scattered on the platform. But the incense and the lamp were burning in front of Jawaharlal.

Would spinning the prayer wheel or *mani* here be the equivalent of intoning some other mantra instead of 'Om Mani Padme Hum'? 'Nehru Padme Hum', perhaps? Seeing my consternation, the aged lama said, 'Nehru Gompa, Nehru Gompa!'

Then he went back outside, followed by the dogs. The yard was uncared for, full of weeds, devoid of grass, goat droppings everywhere. There was a paved spot beneath a large bell, which the lama approached with stately footsteps and rang. Why did he ring it? Its beautiful, solemn sound was echoed by the mountains. I understood nothing.

No bridge of language connected us.

I returned languidly.

The dogs said nothing.

They did not give chase.

The one who's leaving faces no obstacles. On my way back I suddenly heard the sweet sounds of a different sort of bell. Not one, but several. *Ting tong ting tong ting tong.* A female yak emerged from behind a house, a square bell fastened around its throat. The kind of bell I'd seen around the necks of cows in the Tyrol area of the Alps. Then another, and yet another. Two Tibetan dogs were escorting a herd of belled yaks with great responsibility. They would have been called sheepdogs in the West. Prancing behind them, holding a minuscule stick, was an extremely tiny creature wrapped in a dirty, thick baku made of Bhutia blanket material, the tip of her nose covered in green phlegm, her feet encased in Tibetan socks and shoes like strips of coloured ribbons wound around them. She had a face like a freshly bloomed rose. What a lovely housewifely shepherd girl she made. She didn't seem much older than four.

After the sonorous cadences of the bell rung by the lama in the yard of the Nehru Gompa, these little bells had created an air of pleasant melody, partly dispelling the unadorned silence of the morning that had no birdsong.

The doctor's quarters lay in front of me. I found the doctor in the veranda when I entered, a cup of tea in each hand. He began to fuss as soon as he saw me. 'Where did you go? I was worried, it's a new place, what if you got lost?' Alas, would I ever be lost in this uninhabited human habitation even if I wanted to be? No houses, no trees, no people—only rocks. I hadn't yet reached the state where I could blend into the rocks and disappear from sight. Not that that would have been a bad thing.

Once I had taken possession of the doctor like a spirit on a dark night, I made no attempt to move to the Circuit House, for it stood all by itself high on a mountaintop. How was I to find a companion there? Bahadur had already started saying 'Stay a week at least, Memsahib. We never have guests here....' All this had emboldened the doctor too, who was now saying 'No point in your moving out now that I have borrowed the bedding....'

Why should I object? There was no problem—on the contrary, I had found a good friend. The doctor was shy, but he wasn't a bad sort at all. Would he have introduced me to three other doctors even before lunch otherwise? Dr Kar, from whose house the bedding had been borrowed, and Dr Mohanty were both from Orissa, while Dr Gupta was from Bihar.

We had lunch at Dr Kar's house. His wife had made delicious trout curry, dal, rice, and fries.

The person to whom Dr Lalwani introduced me at the hospital after lunch was a surprise. This was the medical officer Dr Swapna Chowdhury, a freshly minted Bengali medical graduate—practically a teenager. She took us to her quarters, where she lived with her widowed mother. Her spick-and-span household appealed to me. The young woman was doing the job of a son. So who was the stern medical officer at the general hospital in this remote land meant for exiles? An unmarried young Bengali woman. I felt my chest swelling with pride on her mother's behalf. Quite naturally, though, they were unable to settle down in this place where they had no family or friends, and were waiting for a transfer. And while I may have been surprised by Swapna's presence there, she and her mother were even more surprised to learn that I had boarded a rations truck to Tawang on a mere whim, without rhyme or reason. Could anyone even *do* such a thing? Not on work, not on assignment, but just like that?

~

Hello, Mrs Lalwani

The doctor took me to the chief engineer's house too, as well as to other senior officers' houses. As we were paying our visits, a jeep stopped on the road.

'Doctor! Hello! Oh, so *this* is why you went home? To fetch Mrs Lalwani! Hello, hello!' A man leapt out of the jeep and ran towards us, jumping up and down and shouting. He looked like he was from the hills, dressed in khaki and a solar hat, though he wasn't in the military. He held his hand out towards me.

'Hello! Pleased to meet you. But I'm not Mrs Lalwani, I'm Dr Sen. And you?'

'Sorry, sorry. I'm Deuri. I thought….'

'You're not the first; many here thought the same thing—it doesn't matter. As long as Dr Lalwani doesn't mind.'

'Our ADC,' the doctor said reverentially. A question mark must have appeared on my face, in response to which someone whispered from the back of the jeep, 'Additional Deputy Commissioner'. Followed by 'Nomoshkar, I'm Subhashranjan Ghosh. I'm the agricultural officer here.'

Immediately afterward I heard myself asking Deuri, 'Can you provide me a jeep? I want to go to the Tawang Gompa. I teach at Jadavpur University. It's impossible to get there without a vehicle….'

'Of course, certainly I'll provide you with a vehicle, but come to our office for a cup of tea first.' Mr Deuri bundled us into his jeep.

A wonderful man. A tribal from this area of Arunachal Pradesh, he was an IAS officer. He had a beautiful office, with modern equipment. A lovely she-dog appeared as soon as we arrived to welcome Deuri rapturously. 'What a pretty dog.'

'Our guard. Our night watchman. Just that she's a little busy these days, having given birth to eight pups. A very powerful watchdog.'

'Eight? May I take one?'

'Of course! Which one would you like? Get them here.'

The bearers fetched eight fluffy balls of cotton at once and released them on the carpet. I picked the plumpest but most animated one. Not today, I would take it with me on the way back. Let it stay with its mother till then.

'Who'll take Dr Sen to see the gompa? You, Mr Ghosh?' So it was decided.

~

Tawang Gompa

I'm not writing a history book. A lot has been written about Tawang Gompa already, and I have no special knowledge to add to it. I'm told that the gompas in Leh–Ladakh are also like this. Enormous, with a number of stone houses on the periphery for people to live in, while the expanse of the gompa lies within the walls. There was a very tall pole inside, painted brightly in different colours, with a huge flag flying from it. There was also a cluster of several poles at one spot outside the walls, with white pennants fluttering on them. I heard that people donated them to ensure peace for the souls of their departed relatives. A massive bell hung outside the gompa. Several young lamas were reading the scriptures inside. A strangely stirring cadence. Even little boys were leaping into the air to ring the bell before entering the gompa.

Student lamas of different ages were studying inside. Aged between eight and eighteen.

But things went wrong while I was trying to view the statue of Buddha inside the main gompa. There was a smaller chamber inside the large one. The 'idol' was placed on the other side of a glass wall. Idol, meaning the statue of Buddha. A huge oil lamp was burning, probably made of brass, for it looked like it was made of gold. Referring to the oil in the lamp, Subhash-babu said, 'Pure yak butter'. There was water in a large silver bowl. But where was the idol? Two legs were arranged in the lotus position on a platform, with the incense, lamp, and water arrayed before them. I peered as closely as I could, but the rest of the Buddha's figure wasn't visible. Subhash-babu said, 'The stairs, you have to take the stairs to see the rest.' Climbing up a floor, I gazed apprehensively at the right hand, palm outwards, signifying protection and overcoming of fear. A headless statue. I wasn't overwhelmed in any way.

The stairs once more.

I had never felt the significance of these two phrases so deeply before. One was 'To be revealed gradually', and the other, 'Head to toe'. The Buddha of Tawang Gompa was the literal embodiment of both these terms. He was 'to be revealed gradually' from 'head to toe'. Climbing the stairs to the second floor allowed us to see his mystic smile and half-closed eyes.

I had seen thirty- or forty-feet-high statues of the Buddha in Sri Lanka too, but those were all in the open air. Even the Jain Mahavir's huge statue at Shravanabelagola is not imprisoned in a gompa like this. The very idea of the feet on the ground floor and the head on the second raises the spectre of a demon, not of the Buddha. None of those other statues reveals itself as an urban tenant occupying the first or the second floor of a building. No, there was no joy to such a viewing.

This was not fulfilling at all. I comprehended the sheer dimensions of the statue, but where was the thrill in my blood? Negotiating the stairs every time meant negotiating heartbreak too. I could have been much more moved if the gigantic brass statue could have been viewed at a single glance, even if from a distance.

I haven't been to China. But in Japan I have seen massive figures of the Buddha inside the temples in Kyoto and in Nara. Beneath very high ceilings, those great statues of the Buddha revealed themselves in their entirety, with breathtaking effect.

The main chamber in this gompa was huge too, but I couldn't tell why the figure of the Buddha had been confined within a separate compartment. What was the need for all this security? A tall, narrow shaft like the ones used for lifts had been constructed for the statue to be placed inside. It was a snug fit. But where in this fragmented view—the hands after the legs, the head after the hands—was the joy of seeing the whole? This was like a comic-strip view of a deity. I got a glimpse, yes, but I might as well not have for all the difference it made. Something remained unfulfilled, like an unquenched thirst.

I hadn't realized earlier why the male lovers in all the literatures of the world want to see the women they love naked. Today I understand, thanks to that fragmented view of the figure of the Buddha in Tawang, that you cannot see the person you love through the folds in their clothes. That kind of viewing does not satisfy the devotee's eye.

On one side was a glass showcase with thousands of statues of the Buddha (possibly made of brass, though they said it was gold). And beyond them, an extraordinary library. I had barely seen three or four original manuscripts like these in my life. Here, there were more than two thousand Buddhist manuscripts, each of them wrapped in yellow fabric and tied with strings. They were laid out with great care, and dusted regularly. These manuscripts did not share the plight of the books languishing in the stacks of our modern libraries. I had not had the fortune of reading such manuscripts. My tutor Sir Harold Bailey's joys would have known no bounds had he been here. He would have been able to decipher them.

Subhash-babu had said that every village in Arunachal had gompas, and that even the village gompas had libraries. I did not explore all those archives. They are stuffed with ingredients for historians, with a great deal of local history stored in them. The British hadn't disturbed them, and the Chinese hadn't looted them. They were all in place. Researchers never used them. I realized that countless myths could be unearthed here, thousands of jewels, a treasury of folklore. They didn't contain the history of the kings and their ministers or of the lamas alone. But I was not prepared. Having arrived without preparation, I could not make use of any of it. But I did wish I could visit a village and stay with a Mompa tribal family.

I presented the idea to Subhash-babu as soon as it occurred to me. With a smile he said, 'Why should it be impossible? Let me try. Allow me to give it some thought.'

~

Ani Gompa

Another white gompa was visible on the peak of a distant mountain. Which one was this?

'That's Ani Gompa. You have to ride a long way up on a mule. There's no motorable road. Nor can you walk; it's too steep.'

'What on earth is Ani Gompa? Is it like Nehru Gompa? Named after someone?'

'No, *ani* means *sanyasini*. Female monks. The Ani Gompa is a monastery for sanyasinis. Men aren't allowed in. In simple terms, a nunnery. There are just two of them in India. One here in Tawang, and the other in Dharamshala, where the Dalai Lama lives. Very rare. If you stay here for a few days, I'll arrange for a mule and send you with Yeshi.

'Who's Yeshi?'

'One of the anis. A friend of ours. Knows Hindi. Belongs to Tawang. She's here now.'

'Really? Can't I meet her?'

'Why not? I'll introduce you today. Her family lives right next door, in the Shiu-basti. Her parents live there. These are not slums though, they're tenements.'

On the way back we went and met Yeshi, the ani, in Shiu-basti. She invited us to lunch the next day. Of course we'd go. What a pretty girl! About nineteen or twenty, she could speak broken Hindi as well as broken English. 'We're female

monks,' Yeshi said with a broad smile. 'We mustn't commit
sins. Women sin quite a lot in any case, but committing a sin
as an ani makes it much worse.' Her face was wreathed in a
childlike smile. The eldest of seven children, she had become
an ani on her parents' instructions. This would mean salvation
for her as well as for them. If you had three sons, it was the
rule to make the second son a lama and send him to a gompa.
There were no such rules for daughters, though—you became
an ani only if you wished to. There were many female monks,
and even children could become anis. Yeshi had been sent to
the gompa at fifteen; she was twenty now.

'What do you do at the monastery when you wake up?'

'We pray. We have to pray. When we wake up we sweep the
floor, light incense sticks, offer water to the Buddha in silver
bowls, drink our tea, and then pray. We pray a little less on the
days we have more work to do. After prayers, breakfast. Roti
or jau or halwa. We have to collect the rations from the *basti*,
work the mill to make flour from wheat; there's so much to do.
We have a lot of tasks.

'Money? No, we have no money. Others pay for us. They
give me some money at home too every time I visit. Forty of us
anis live in the gompa. We cook in groups of three or four once
a fortnight. We pray morning and evening. We study too.'

Five or six junior anis were assigned to one senior ani, who
taught them the Tibetan language, and how to read the manuscripts. Studies went on all day. There was one head ani, who
kept the keys. The keys to the scriptures. What other keys
could an ani possibly have?

And yes, many things were 'forbidden' for anis. For instance,
'Do not lie. Do not steal, do not marry, do not fall in love, do
not do anything with a man, not even talk to one. If you do,
if you are seen moving about with anyone, you'll get a bad

name. People will say you've fallen in love. Still some of the anis run away when they find someone; they run away from the gompa, and they get married.' They had to pay a fine, though. They had to bribe the anis and lamas with tea.

An elaborate prayer ceremony was conducted for those who did not run away, after they had spent three or four years as monks. Their relatives and fellow villagers pooled some money for this, each paying a thousand or five hundred or a hundred rupees, depending on their means. After this they became full-fledged anis or lamas.

~

The Inimical Number Three

All these conversations took place at a tea shop on the edge of Shiu-basti, over Tibetan salt tea. Yesterday too I had tried this concoction in tea rooms while wandering around with the doctor. So I had already learnt the art of the Tibetan tea ceremony. Charming, round, black wooden bowls whose outer sides were inlaid with brass and copper plates and colourful patterns of beads. The tea was like nothing I'd ever tasted before.

I'd drunk tea at dhabas, tea of the kind measured out in feet, even yards (small and strong), jasmine-flavoured Chinese tea, Japanese tea that had to be drunk while squatting on your haunches, holding the bowl in both hands, green, with a wild flavour, and (no matter how stylishly served) a wild taste too. I'd drunk the tea brewed by monks at the Kumbh Mela as offerings to the gods, almost like the Bengali *paayesh* with the taste of full cream and flavoured with cinnamon and carda-mom. But Tibetan tea could not be compared to any of this. The first taste was a numbing surprise. It felt like a profound betrayal. I was almost in tears. I always considered myself the world's worst tea maker. But the entire Tibetan race had left me behind.

I was a bit surprised by Atish Dipankar Srijnan's taste too. I had heard tales that the first recorded Bengali words in Tibet were *'Bhalo, bhalo, khub bhalo'*. (Good, good, very good.) A wise man like Atish Dipankar had uttered these enchanted words after drinking Tibetan tea for the first time. So, this was it?

It was awfully salty. Laced with ghee, smelling of fish, oily on the surface. Much of it, of course, was due to the unexpectedness of it all. It was very difficult to drink this tea. But the doctor said I had to finish it. Wasting it was tantamount to an insult. Even at the tea shop. The aluminium teapot resembled a very large rosewater can, shaped like an earthen pitcher. A pretty young girl with body odour and a world-conquering smile was pouring tea from it. None of us understood one another's language. Every time she poured the tea, she set the pitcher down with a thud on the floor afterwards, picking it up again to pour. This was the system. My stomach churned as I emptied my bowl, but the young woman refilled my bowl every time with a sweet smile. With great sympathy the doctor whispered, 'There's no choice. You have to drink it thrice. That's the rule. These people are very ritualistic. They always follow the rules. There's nothing bad in there; after all, it's all healthy. Yak butter, yak milk, salt, and tea. That's all there is. Might as well as drink it up. When in Rome. You can't waste it, you see, the hosts will feel insulted.' The third bowl appeared as soon as I finished my second. It took me over an hour to finish it. It was, however, accompanied by a dry namkeen, oily jalebis, and biscuits. This was breakfast on my first morning in Tawang. That was when I learnt to drink salt tea. It was made by grinding the leaves in a wooden mortar a couple of feet tall, an elegant device.

Anyhow, I didn't allow myself to be fooled at the Shiu-basti tea shop. I drank the first cup comfortably, but became apprehensive once I was done with it. 'Oh no, two cups more.' As soon as I blurted this out Subhash-babu said, laughing, 'You'd better learn the trick. Put the cup on the floor after a few sips. They'll still refill it. Then do the same thing again. They'll refill it once more. A cup and a half will do the job of three servings. You won't break the ritual, but you'll protect your stomach. But then you know what, you'll get used to it in a day or two. It won't taste bad anymore; it's the yak butter that gives it the fishy smell. I quite enjoy Tibetan tea now.'

'Ten years in Tibet must have made you half-Tibetan.'

~

Beyond Reach

'Oh my god! Stop calling it Tibet, Madam, this is India. Can't you see all the "Our India" posters everywhere?'

'Take a look at these placards saying *We're proud to be Indian*—Have you seen anything like this in Calcutta? Or in Delhi? Is there any doubt that culturally this is Tibet? The people here belong to a Tibetan tribe; their language is Tibetan, their food, their clothes, their habits, their religion are all Tibetan. Even the cows and goats and cats and dogs over here are Tibetan, Tibetan hounds, Lhasa Apsos, yaks— and you still say this isn't Tibet?'

'You're a nuisance, Madam. You write poetry and things. You have no idea of politics or history or anthropology. Don't you understand that mere Tibetan culture doesn't make this Tibet? Jalpaiguri was part of Bhutan till 1860 or 1870—does that mean it's part of Bhutan even today? Darjeeling belonged to Sikkim till thirty years or so before that—does that mean it still belongs to Sikkim? Then why should Tawang be in Tibet? Are you going to make the same claims as China?'

It was true. I had spoken like an ignorant fool. And dangerously, too! I changed the topic.

'Have you met the Chinese?'

'How would I? I came here only in 1967. But I've seen the road that the Chinese built, the Lhasa–Tawang Road. They constructed the road in just ten days. It's incredible. There's been no sign of any maintenance for fifteen years, but it's in perfect shape. There's absolutely no problem taking a jeep.

'What a beautiful area it is! You can travel about ten miles along the road beyond the border, no one stops you. We went on a picnic with the ADC's permission. There's a wonderful blue lake, filled with swans.' What! Really? 'I want to go, I want to go,' I demanded at once. When that didn't work, I tried even more intensely, saying, 'Let's go without telling anyone.' But still no luck. Unmoved, Subhashranjan said, 'You can't go at a moment's notice. You need permission.' Still, he was kind enough to take me for a drive along the dream road. A clean, broad, high-altitude road heading north-east towards the eternal mystery of Lhasa. And that was where it lay, beyond reach—the McMahon Line.

'The Lhasa–Tawang Road?' said Mr Sehgal. 'An extraordinary example of engineering.'

We were chatting over a meal at Chief Engineer Mr Sehgal's house that night. The men were also involved with cards and rum on the wide bed. Both of the Sehgals' children were on the same bed, refusing to go to sleep, giggling and throwing sidelong glances at the others. They went to school here in Tawang. Mrs Sehgal was very keen that they go to a good boarding school once they were a little grown up.

'The Lhasa–Tawang Road was built by a woman.' It was Mrs Sehgal who said it.

'What? Really?'

'Yes, a twenty-six-year-old Chinese woman, an army engineer. She's the one who built it.'

The chief engineer said, clearly excited, 'You wouldn't believe it unless you saw it with your own eyes. A road as good as this, at this altitude, made with whatever material was at hand. And how long did it take? Just ten days. What was the road for? Heavy vehicles. Tanks and so on. This Lhasa–Tawang Road is an incredible achievement. Local people from the hills were employed to line the swampy stretches with rocks. Once the soil was firm, wooden beams were laid down at right angles. The road was constructed with these beams. They had cut all the wood they needed from trees on the way, carrying it themselves, since this area is above the tree line, without much vegetation. They had cut down trees from the valley over there to make wooden beams. All of it the brain-child of that one young woman.'

That was the famous McMahon Line. Part of the Tawang border subdivision, Kameng District, at altitudes ranging from 4,000 to 19,000 feet. Right next door, Lumla village stands on the Bhutan–Tibet border. On the other side of the Tse-La is the Bum-La, which is the road to Bhutan. Even higher than the Tse-La Pass. I had a powerful urge to go to the Bum-La and continue to Bhutan—but there was no time. My holidays were ending. The college would reopen soon.

I wasn't really a free bird; I might not be chained, but I was still tethered to the rod. I may not have been caged, but I had to keep going back. That was where my food and water awaited me. And besides, even the free bird had a nest to return to, where its scarlet chicks were waiting with their beaks parted.

Freedom is never guaranteed. The lord himself is bound to everyone by his act of creation. And we are subservient crea-tures. We take wing, but we come back too.

'Didn't you say you wanted to visit a Tibetan village? This is Lama Pemma Khandu; you can stay at his house if you like. He can speak Hindi.' A handsome young lama accompanying Subhash-babu was saying 'Namaste' to me. It was soon settled that a jeep would take me to his little village, whose name was

Chomprung, that afternoon. Pemma Khandu himself would receive me there. He would have to go home at once to inform his family. The poor fellow was visiting the ADC's office on some business, and had been waylaid by Subhash-babu. Since the ADC was not in Tawang today, he wouldn't have got anywhere in any case. I was ecstatic. Lunch at Yeshi-ani's house, dinner at Lama Pemma Khandu's house. At least I'd get a glimpse of the 'Tibetan way of life'. I'd also learn something about the way lamas and anis lived.

~

STD!

Yeshi-ani was waiting for me in front of their house in Shiu-basti. She took us upstairs, her face dazzling with a happy smile. One large room downstairs, and a small one on the first floor. All Tibetan houses had just these two rooms. The lower one was for work and living, and the upper, for prayers. It was also where the children studied, and guests were seated.

The entire household fitted into the room downstairs—cooking, eating, resting, sleeping. The one upstairs was always spick and span, and secluded. A tiny mezzanine room. Her father was waiting there for us. He greeted us and offered us seats. Yeshi's younger brothers and sisters appeared constantly to peep at us. Three of us had been invited—the doctor, Subhash-babu, and I. The doctor had been on duty in the morning. He was picked up before lunch from his 'STD Clinic'.

'Can you explain what this STD Clinic is? I know there's a telephone STD service nowadays—is this something to do with telephones too?' Suddenly I found the doctor blushing like he used to earlier. He had turned cherry red. What was it?

Subhash-babu wasn't speaking either.

Not that anyone addressed him as Subhash-babu, but I had insisted. Everyone else called him Mr Ghosh. All that 'babu' business was out of place here. It was a military area, after all. There were not even any regular policemen for civilians here, only the Central Reserve Police. Hmmph!

Still, I continued to address him as Subhash-babu. I am sometimes possessed by a disgusting, unsophisticated Bengali spirit. I simply cannot stand 'Mr So and So'.

'What *is* it? What *is* this STD Clinic?'

'Have I made a mistake asking this question? Why?'

'Is it some sort of secret military code? In that case, never mind. But why doesn't one of you say something?'

Exasperated by my barrage of questions, Subhash-babu finally said, 'It's a clinic for venereal diseases.'

'I see. But that's called VD, isn't it? What does STD mean?'

'VD is out of fashion now. The new term is "sexually transmitted disease". STD.'

This time it was the doctor who answered, after clearing his throat and straightening his collar. Oh lord, here you are treating this disease every day, and you still blush without reason, and you cannot go to sleep if there's a woman in the same room? It was tragic, the punishment meted out to this man for the sake of earning a living.

The conversation should be continued. So I said, 'Is STD rampant here?'

'Of course. There are just four main diseases here. Worms, leprosy, VD, and TB. The mountain people fall prey to them often.'

'My goodness! All four are bad, aren't they? No quick cures.'

'VD can be cured by penicillin, and TB by streptomycin. Those two are relatively under control these days. But worms and leprosy, not yet....'

Yeshi-ani brought us a warm white drink in bowls with Chinese motifs, arranged on a patterned lacquer tray.

'Sing chhang,' said Subhash-babu. 'Appetizer.'

'Alcohol?'

'Sort of. Think of it as wine. Harmless. Even the children drink it here. It's a ritual, keeps them warm. Like tea. A kind of filtered beer, basically.'

The sing chhang didn't taste bad at all. Our bowls were refilled. Thrice in this case too. The doctor and Mr Ghosh may not have minded several more refills instead of stopping at three, but the food arrived. Momos and thukpa. The warm sing chhang was a lot like the Japanese sake. Quite delicious, though not too strong.

A sudden revelation struck me like a bolt of lightning. Atish Dipankar Srijnan couldn't possibly have made his appreciative comment after drinking Tibetan tea—it must have been in response to chhang. But a middle-class Bengali, who was moreover a respected scholar, had a reputation to be protected. So we Bengalis must have decided to pass it off as tea instead of chhang when recounting the history. The very idea of such an erudite man becoming ecstatic about a strange-tasting drink and offering repeated, gratified praise was shocking. But for chhang, it is quite a suitable comment.

The momos were stuffed with boiled yak meat and served with chilli sauce, while the thukpa was full of meat and vegetables. Both were delicious. Yeshi's mother kept serving us on a tray, while the smiling children looked on from the door.

'Aren't they eating?'

'They ate a long time ago.'

Yeshi's father was eating with us, but neither Yeshi nor her mother were.

'When will you eat?'

'After you're done.'

I'd been told Yeshi had six brothers and sisters, but not all of them were to be seen. There were just three or four little things trotting about.

Yeshi was quite grown-up, but her eyes held the simplicity of a child's. She spoke of good and evil very seriously, and looked quite transformed when she did.

'Why don't anis marry? Yeshi? I heard lamas do.'

'The junior lamas marry, but not the senior ones. They live in the gompas; they have no homes. The anis live in the gompas too. Those who live in gompas do not marry. It's a rule for anis to remain virgins. Marrying is a sin.'

'What about those who run away and get married? Didn't you tell us? What happens to them?'

'Nothing at all. They're only fined. And not allowed to live in gompas anymore. And they have to treat all the anis from their gompa to tea.'

'The other consequences came "after death".'

'Why, what happens after death?'

'It's a sin, of course. This makes it difficult to arrive in god's land. One day's sin can cancel an entire lifetime of piety—you might even have to be reborn as a worm. You will definitely be born as a yak; even a life as a snake is possible.' In sum, Yeshi had no doubt that terrible punishments were inevitable.

'Have you seen the Getompa?' Yeshi-ani asked me. 'In the Tawang Gompa?'

'No. What's the Getompa?'

'What's the Getompa?' Subhash-babu then replied. 'Eight large volumes, containing Buddhadeva's life and instructions. Three of the volumes are written in actual gold letters. They're from Tibet, kept in this gompa. But they probably don't let everyone see them.'

Besides the main temple, there were also smaller stupas, temples, and some tantric figures in the compound of the Tawang Gompa. I had been wandering around, looking at them. The poky little rooms, like prison cells, the dingy lanes, an aged woman devotee bent over from the waist, sweeping the ground, another one with glasses threshing and winnowing some grain with a squarish colander. The Shiu-basti began on the other side of the gompa, with its alleys and tap-yards, its poverty, and its inhabitants' shops and lives.

That afternoon a young man interviewed me briefly for Tawang Radio. What had the journey to Tawang on a truck been like? Where had I been educated? What did I do now? What did I read? What did I write? The radio station was a little higher, on top of a desolate hill, the wooden building in which it was housed resembling army barracks.

From the radio station Subhash-babu took me to the Tawang Arts and Crafts Centre, where Kamaladevi Chattopadhay had found her three-day visit to inaugurate the place turning into a sojourn of several weeks on the heights of Tawang. The carpet factory here was well and truly worth a visit. Not a single carpet was available for sale. All of them were still being woven, which took time. Marvellous Tibetan wool carpets with ancient Chinese designs of flowers and vines and dragons and swastikas in dazzling colours. They would send me a carpet if I ordered one, so I did. It would take three months to be woven, and at least another month to be delivered. (That carpet never did arrive. Nor did the colour photographs promised by the doctor and Subhash-babu.)

Beside carpets, all kinds of wooden objects were also being crafted—flower vases and ashtrays were being made and coloured. Exquisite! Such wondrously dazzling dragons were being painted on in black and red and gold and green. I bought several. Even the plain ones, without any designs on them, were beautiful, made as they were of gorgeous white wood. I was very tempted to buy a lovely little device for making salt tea, but Subhash-babu advised me against it, saying, 'You won't have any use for it.' That was true. I would have bought the teapot resembling a rosewater sprinkler if I had found one, though. It wasn't available. There were bukharis of different sizes, and incense. I was told handmade paper was a distinctive craft of the region, but I couldn't buy any. Wooden bowls were being painted in one room. An old Tibetan and several teenage Tibetans were sitting in a cosy circle with paint and brushes. I was astonished to see that they were using Camel poster colours. The bowls were being painted and then coated with copal varnish. Just like we did at home in Calcutta. But the same colours in Tawang? I was very disappointed. I had heard that it was the custom to use local pigments, made from the earth. But how could an elaborate commercial venture from the government follow that rule? It could only work in villages.

~

The Return Journey

Leaving his clinic, the doctor picked me up in his jeep. Now for the return journey. Gather up your bundle, traveller. This trip was to Champrung Village, where Lama Pemma Ge aka Pemma Khandu was waiting for me. Subhash-babu said, 'We'll meet tomorrow afternoon.' Everything was settled. They would pick me up at Chámprung and take me all the way to Tezpur in an Agriculture Department bus. There was a meeting there, which three or four of them were going to attend. It would be a simple matter to stop at Champrung on the way, since everyone knew Pemma Ge's gompa.

'What about my puppy?'

'Don't worry, I'll bring it with me. You can't take it to Champrung after all. Where will you put it? You'll be staying in the gompa room.'

'What on earth is that?'

'Every house here has two rooms, right? One to live in and one for prayers. Guests are put up in the prayer room. That's why.'

'Very well, I'll go on ahead then. Let the puppy come later.'

'Yes, it's settled.'

'Don't forget....'

Subhash-babu smiled. 'Let me drop you at the doctor's place.'

I was packing when my hand encountered something solid. What was this? I was terrified suddenly. It felt like a bomb.

Something round. I pulled everything out of my suitcase and flung them to the floor. A pair of bombs emerged in the process.

Two tins of Milkmaid condensed milk. My tears wouldn't stop.

Behind the doctor's shy, awkward, distant, disinterested behaviour, there was an affection and warmth that revealed themselves now and then. This time, though, they had surrendered without any attempt at camouflage, in the form of those two tins of condensed milk.

The doctor had bought brandy and condensed milk in Jung the night we arrived at Tawang. They came cheap if friends in the military bought them for you. I love licking condensed milk off a spoon. As soon as the tin was opened to make tea, I had asked Bahadur for a spoonful and was savouring it slowly. The doctor's mouth fell open. What was this? A double MA, PhD, FRAS, mother of two grown-up girls, chief guest ... licking condensed milk off a spoon. Embarrassed by the astonishment in his eyes, I began to babble, 'I love this more than rasgullas or gulab jamuns, you see. We grew up in a time of war, you know. That's when our taste buds developed and our greed took root. To tell you the truth, this tastes like *rabri* to me.'

I don't know whether the explanation appealed to the doctor, but he fetched the tin and refilled my spoon.

To tell the truth, it wasn't as though I hadn't tasted any condensed milk at all over the few days that had passed since then. But there had been no conversation with the doctor about it. I had no trouble identifying the person who had slipped the two tins into my bags without my knowledge. Can you blame my tears? How could my heart not echo this unexpected clarion call of Bengali maternal sentiment in a shy young Sindhi man?

Bahadur was forlorn. Just three days? When will you be back? Never? How can that be? Who goes on such a difficult journey for such a short time?

'We thought the new madam has been transferred and is moving here. In place of the old madam. That's what they were saying at the tea shop. Look, the new madam is here.'

'Who's the old madam?' I asked with deep suspicion.

'Nothing to do with me,' the doctor answered hurriedly. 'She's been transferred. She was the DC, Miss Neeru Nanda, IAS. An extremely honest and hardworking lady. She was popular with everyone.'

'A young woman. She did a lot of work around the villages. She began peach and apple farming here, and encouraged potato farming too. Though that had started earlier, we supply potatoes to your Sealdah Market and to cold storages.' This was clearly the respected Agriculture Officer of Tawang. With the conversation veering round to apples, his face had turned as rosy as one.

'Ah, now I understand all those salutes and the "Huzoor Memsahib" treatment you were getting at the Jamiri IB.'

Suddenly, the doctor spoke in an uncharacteristically loud voice.

'Just like Bahadur's friends they too must have thought this is the new madam replacing the old one, or why should she be giving so many orders? Get the cot in there, unlock the drawing room … my god! What a towering personality! I was astounded when you got the chowkidar to make tea for you at that hour of the night!'

The doctor suddenly shrank. A rare outburst. Or perhaps he had remembered the spoonfuls of condensed milk. Oh yes, quite a personality!

I changed the subject with Subhash-babu.

'Where is Neeru Nanda now?'

'In Delhi, with her father in Vasant Vihar. I'll give you her address; in case you happen to visit Delhi you must tell her about us. Tell her everyone here still loves her, respects her, that they remember her. Tell her we miss her a *lot.*'

My gratitude to Neeru Nanda knew no bounds. I had never met her, but I was reaping the full benefits of all that she had sowed. I think it was the love and respect for 'DC Memsahib' among the Mompas in the mountains of Champrung and Tundrala villages that they diverted generously to another independent woman. After all, I was a stranger, who had done nothing at all for them. The way they accepted me as one of their own, like a member of the family, was not insignificant at all. The locals were charmed. Since outsiders didn't visit very often, they were not used to mingling with others, and were wracked by doubts about them. They neither embraced anyone instantly as one of their own, nor trusted them. I didn't know what similarities Bahadur had found between me and the 'Old Madam', but I was sure that that was the reason the Mompas gave me the same kind of love that they would normally give only to someone in the family.

No one had quite expected this. The Indian officers visiting Tawang had all been surprised at my unreasonable demand of living with a Mompa family in their home. Perhaps they were a little annoyed too. Wasn't I overdoing things? They were very dirty, they didn't bathe, they were infested with lice, their food was inedible—'Don't imagine you'll get Chinese food (considering what their tea was like)'—they were extremely poor; on top of which I didn't know their language, and they weren't used to social interaction. True, they weren't a thieving race, and they were very courteous, but still, why not give up this wild idea and travel around the villages in a jeep instead? But I wasn't to be distracted from my mission. I had already finalized things with Pemma Khandu in the morning. I would go, and go today. In the afternoon. To Chomprung Village.

~

Lama Mia!

Pemma Ge was indeed waiting by the road when our jeep arrived. The doctor got off and escorted me and my luggage to Pemma Ge's house. It was quite high, up several flights of steps cut into the hillside. The doctor did not stay, for he had to release the jeep.

'See you later, bye.' The doctor turned round abruptly.

'When? Where? Thank you, Shyamsundar, how would I have managed in this foreign land without a brother like you?'

'You'd have found someone else. You will never lack for companions.'

'I'm leaving tomorrow….'

'We'll meet again. Take care, good luck.'

'How? Where?'

'I'm sure we will, somewhere or the other….' The doctor practically ran off towards his jeep. It disappeared up the winding road. When will we meet again, Doctor? Where?

'This is my gompa. I am the lama here,' said Pemma in Hindi. 'My eldest son is a lama too; he's eighteen. His gompa is in another village. You can see it over there.' He pointed at a spot in the distance, a little lower than where we were. Chomprung was lower than Tawang. There were many trees here. Evening had gathered in the orchard. In front of us, on the slopes below, was another habitation, and there, the roof of a gompa was visible. It was lit up by the setting sun.

Pemma announced proudly, 'My son is the lama of *that* gompa.'

Darkness was playing hide-and-seek with the lamp and the candles in the gompa room. The aromatic fragrance of the incense automatically made you want to pray. A soft, thick, beautifully patterned carpet lined the floor. In the sanctum within the room was the figure of the meditating Buddha. But it wasn't him alone. Several unfamiliar figures of Tibetan gods and goddesses also stood against the wall. In front of the Buddha was a lamp burning yak butter. Quite a few thick candles were burning before them. Everyone from Bhim to Bhairav were glaring at me, their teeth bared. Large figures of brass. The human-sized gods and goddesses were not beautiful at all—I felt exquisitely pretty in comparison. (I also felt a sensation of self-pity à la Sita in Ashok Vatika surrounded by her rakshasi entourage.) I tried to tear my eyes away from them to chat with Pemma Ge, but they refused to reciprocate, their bulging eyes boring into me.

Pemma was forty, and his wife, fifty-four. They had been twenty and thirty-four, respectively, when they got married. His parents had chosen his bride. His father had been a lama too, and so had his grandfather.

Pemma had seen his grandparents, who were dead now, as were his parents. 'My wife is an old woman now,' Pemma said regretfully. 'Fourteen years older, after all.' Why had his parents chosen a bride so much older than him? 'She was a good girl, hardworking. She looked after my aged parents, that's why.'

'Isn't she a good girl anymore? Doesn't she look after you?'

'She does. She works very hard, looks after the children, tends to the garden.'

'How many children?'

'One son, a lama. Three daughters. The eldest is named Kindar Khamo. She's seventeen, does all the housework. The second one is fourteen. She's an ani, and lives in a gompa. And the youngest is eight, she goes to school. Her name is Urakin Khamo.'

'How did you learn so much Hindi?'

'In India. I've been to India many times. Three times to Dharamshala, to bow before the Dalai Lama. Twice to Delhi on Republic Day. Just four years ago I went to Bodhgaya, and Kullu–Manali too—I've been to India many times, you see.'

While Pemma chattered happily, I thought to myself, poor Government of India. Despite all the 'This is Mother India' and 'Proud to be an Indian' posters, the government hasn't been able to regulate the language of the people here. What sort of statement was 'I've been to India'? What would the Chinese say if they heard? And Pakistan?

'Ten of us from Chomprung-basti went to Kullu–Manali for training in apple-farming and apple-pruning. We stayed four months, January to April, so I learnt how to speak Hindi. In Kullu, in a place named Thanadar, I saw that each farmer owned two hundred acres of orchards each, can you believe it? No one here has that kind of land. Lamas don't have any land at all. Nor yaks. They only have horses, because they have to travel a lot.'

'What kind of man is the Dalai Lama? Did he talk to you?'

'A very nice man. I went to him after my mother died. To make a donation in her memory, to offer prayers to the Dalai Lama. He's such a wonderful person. He served us food and tea. He listens to you with great attention. As I was leaving he said, travel safely, there are bandits on this road. Twenty-five of us lamas went to meet him and pray to him. We came back happy.' An exquisitely beautiful teenage girl appeared at the door while we were talking, saying something in Tibetan. It was dark outside by now.

The lama told me, 'My eldest daughter, Kindar Khamo. She's asking whether you'll eat here or back at the house. I'll walk you back here afterwards.'

'Oh no, why should I come back here? Who wants to stay alone here at night?' Amidst all these terrifying gods and goddesses, Buddhadeva's was the only familiar face.

'Why don't I go back home with you? I can eat there and sleep there too. Can't I sleep by Kindar Khamo?'

'Of course you can. But you'll find it difficult to sleep there. We're poor people. This gompa is the lama's guestroom. You'll be more comfortable here.'

'Who needs more comfort? I can't possibly spend the entire night with all these gods and goddesses. They'll make me feel like I'm in heaven. I'd rather stay with humans.'

'Then come with me.' Lama Pemma Khandu picked up my suitcase.

Pemma Ge's home was a short walk away after climbing down the stairs from the gompa. There was a prayer wheel outside the front door. I'd seen this in front of everyone's house here. People stepped into their homes only after spinning the wheel to inform god in advance that yes, by your grace, I've finished my day's work and am back home, glory be to you. I liked this system every much. I would have made similar arrangements at home if possible. If not outside the front door at least outside the dining room. So that one could send a prayer up to the god of the home every day before entering the room. I only take recourse to the god who dispels all dangers when I am in trouble, but I never think of the god of all joys when happy. God should put me in trouble all the time if he wants me to think of him. So the prayer wheel is a suitable arrangement for people like me. 'I love god but I don't care for rituals'—there must be many more such unfortunate people in the world.

Spinning the prayer wheel also made a lovely tinkling sound. Each of us spun it once before crossing the threshold of the house into the yard. Beyond the yard you had to climb on to a wooden veranda (without a roof). Then you had to step over a high doorsill made of stone, bowing your head to enter through a low door into a room like a cave. The doors had to be low to keep the cold out. The people here were not very short. Not tall either, of course, but Pemma and his daughter could be said to be tall by Bengali standards.

A gloriously beautiful woman welcomed us with a smile as we entered.

'Karmo, my wife.' She was having a drink of some sort. One of her arms was covered down to the fingertips by her sleeve. My god, was this the woman referred to as old by her ungrateful husband? She wasn't old at all. True, she had wrinkles on her forehead, but in the radiance on her face, in her sparkling teeth, in her smiling eyes, and in the structure of her body, she was definitely a young woman. She didn't appear a day older than thirty-five or perhaps forty. Just that Pemma Ge looked about twenty-five. He didn't seem remotely like the father of his pretty daughter.

There was one more person in the room—a young man with a shaven head, yet to grow facial hair, with a rather tender, sweet face. He offered a shy smile as soon as our eyes met. I was startled by the smile. This was not a man's smile. She had to be a girl.

'My daughter. She's an ani. She came home from the gompa today because she's not well.' She was going back the next day. My heart twisted at her lovely smile. Was this girl going to remain a virgin all her life, her head shaven? Yeshi-ani did have a head of hair, though cut like a man's. The fourteen-year-old girl was as tall as her mother, and as beautiful. She looked like a boy monk.

A lovely mother, surrounded by her daughters, occupying the centre of her impeccable household like Goddess Lakshmi, awaiting her husband, the lama. She was warming herself at the fire, counting her beads, and sipping raksi. It was a pleasant scene. So relaxed. A serene moment, devoid of anxiety. A wide smile on seeing us. And then getting to her feet to prepare for dinner. A housewife, after all.

~

Do Not Go into the Dark, Girl

Meanwhile I needed to go to the bathroom. The more I said this to the girl, the more she smiled. This was annoying. Was there no way to go to the bathroom? This was a human habitation; how could I go out to the fields? Did they even have bathrooms, or did they rely on open spaces? I could make no sense of it. Eventually I swallowed my embarrassment and asked Mr Lama, 'Where is the bathroom?' He asked, 'What's a *battoon*?' Oh my god. 'Latrine? Where's the latrine?'

'*Lattin*? What's a lattin?'

Now what! All the other synonyms I knew were even more of a mouthful, even more remote. Powder-room, toilet, WC, loo, john, little room, lavatory—none of these would work.

'*Shouchagar*? Where's the shouchagar?'

'*Chou … kya*? I don't know. Chou … what?'

Oh lord. Only one particular word would work. Ugh. Being born civilized was no small cross to bear. What we said was not what we meant. It was like having a ten-ton chain wrapped around my tongue. Finally I managed to utter that one sure-fire word, though it sounded less horrible in Hindi. The original was Persian, but it had become a four-letter word in Bangla.

Actually, the word looks just as bad in Bangla as it sounds. About twelve years ago they made me line up for a health check at the immigration queue in London. That was where I saw, for the first time, in bold black letters next to an arrow, the Bangla word *paaykhana*. Following the arrow I did spot an arrangement in the Indian style. What had not materialized despite two hundred years of the Empire had come to pass, thanks to the unhygienic habits of uneducated immigrants from East Pakistan. Spotting a notice in Bangla in the capital of England should have made the heart dance like a plumed peacock. But alas, this *lutice* was the sort that, far from making my heart dance, made me want to run away. If I had to see just one Bangla word in a foreign land, did it have to be this one?

That was how I had felt then. But today I realized the value of that sign. Finally I understood how the poor East Pakistani must have felt, caught in that mousetrap of nature's call without knowing the local language. The word must have brought much peace to some minds at certain moments.

Even Pemma Ge knew this particular Hindi word. He jumped to his feet and ushered me out into the yard. On the way towards the main entrance, Pemma's daughter unlatched the door of a small wooden chamber on the left. Now the lama pronounced the Hindi word with great reverence, as though displaying the Rashtrapati Bhavan to a foreign diplomat.

To be honest I hadn't expected a full-fledged, covered bathroom with a door. Practically indoors. Lovely! About to waltz in, I banged my head on the low doorframe. Just as I was about to enter the darkness within, rubbing my bruise, a sudden onslaught of fear sent my heart into free fall. There was no ground beneath my feet, which had landed on a yawning emptiness. Clutching at the door to regain my balance, I switched on my torch. But before that, for a fraction of a moment, I had experienced the extreme fear of death.

The fear of death is very complex, and very simple at the same time. I suffer from serious respiratory trouble, which means I have an intimate relationship with the agony of dying. I had assumed I couldn't possibly be afraid of death anymore. How could I, when every breath could be my last, when there were times that an overwhelming prayer rose from my heart— let this breath be the final one, my lord, my god.

Whether it is joy or sorrow, life has been bountiful in handing me all its riches. I can now abdicate without any complaints. Those who have families often feel their fear of death is not for themselves. 'What will happen to my children if I die?' That is not what worries me. I am responsible for my children as long as I am alive. How does it matter to me once I'm dead? He who gave me life will take care of this too. I am merely a tool in his hands. I have learnt one very important lesson. Nothing is held up in anyone's life because of someone else. There is no such thing as 'indispensable' or 'unbearable loss' to impede the flow of existence. If I were to disappear from the world today, no one's life will stop eventually. All losses become bearable.

But, arriving as it had without warning, the fear of death made me aware of its intensity. When I opened the door in the dark to step into a deep, bottomless chasm, when my feet were sinking into a void with no support, I felt in my bones what it's like to be at the mercy of your lifespan. 'No ground beneath my feet' often appears as a metaphor, but how often does it make such a crude and literal entry?

It lasted an instant.

I clutched at the door in a moment to stop myself from falling, lighting the torch and planting my foot on the safety of the doorsill.

A row of planks was laid out on the floor before me. Sometimes they were a foot apart, sometimes six inches. The room was wide, but not long. There were hens in baskets inside. Hens or roosters? They clucked a welcome. These weren't the same ones that were in the back of Mr Sen's truck, were they? By the light of the torch I discovered a pile of leaves in the hole running beneath the planks. The entire room had been built like a bridge over a huge pit. Each of the planks was perfectly clean. There was no special opening for specific purposes. No arrangement for water, and certainly no toilet paper. No dust, leaves, or earth. This would be difficult.

How did these people clean up?

Or didn't they?

Wasn't there something called ablution?

Luckily I always have toilet paper in my bag. So I could still manage, but what about them? Worrying deeply about hygiene, I banged my head again when leaving.

I had felt fear twice on the same evening. Once, at the possibility of spending the night in the company of the tantric gods and goddesses in Chomprung Gompa, and now, on stepping into a bottomless pit on opening the bathroom door. I had no other memories of fear during the entire trip.

~

Now That's a Feast

Karmo had prepared dinner in this short span of time. Paa, jhyan, tea, and raksi.

Paa was a sort of curry, made with something similar to water spinach or *kolmi-saak*, yak fat (which they called *chhurpi*), yak butter, and cream. Cooked with salt and chillies, it was delicious. Instead of rice or rotis, Tibetans ate something called jhyan. Pemma said, 'It's boiled pumpkin.' Salt tea and alcoholic raksi were simmering in two samovar-like vessels on the oven. Before pouring the raksi into cups the housewife stirred in a raw egg, which changed its colour to a yellowish white. It tasted partly like eggnog, partly like brandy. Quite tasty.

Raksi was made with rice, pumpkin, and wheat. The lamas did not drink it, and nor did children. But all mothers did. They were the ones who brewed it at home. Chhang, too. Sing chhang was made with rice and pumpkin, without wheat. Subhash-babu had likened it to filtered beer. I didn't get the similarity when drinking sing chhang. Beer is bitter, I hate its taste. Sing chhang wasn't bitter at all. Then why call it beer?

I had my fill of raksi, tea, paa, and jhyan. Then we sat down to chat near the fire. The lama did all the talking. Karmo couldn't join in, since she didn't know my language. Their youngest daughter Urakin Khamo was unbelievably sweet, exactly like a Japanese doll. Chinese-cut hair, apple-cheeked, dressed like her mother and sisters. She kept smiling. During dinner a plump, grave, grey cat appeared, taking a seat like the chairperson of the proceedings. His name was Shimpu. There was no bar on Shimpu's entering the house, but someone else who sat down outside the doorstep, frequently wagging his short tail, was 'not allowed to come in'. He was a Bhutia dog, his eyes covered with fur, named Chottu. Both of them were grey, roly-poly, and adorable. But Chottu was not as vainglorious as Shimpu, relegated in class on account of being denied entry. He could not be treated like an equal.

I discovered in the course of conversation that the Mompas had a strong caste system. There were six castes in all. They had no Baniyas or Kshatriyas, but they had a caste of peasants, and another of painters—the thanka-makers. But only three or four castes lived in Tawang Valley—not all six. What about Tibet? There were other castes there—those who made statues, those who made books, and many more. Even the lamas had their own caste system. The 'pure lamas' were those who did not marry, practising celibacy and living in the gompa, while the 'family lamas' were a different caste, who ran the gompas in villages, but lived in their own households. People from all castes could become lamas, except the two lowest castes—butchers and blacksmiths. Cobblers and potters were low caste too, but they were allowed to touch the water that the others drank—they weren't untouchable. There was no obstacle to their becoming lamas. But Yaps and Sheipas, who made iron tools and horseshoes, and those who slaughtered animals and sliced their meat, were not allowed into Mompa society. They lived in a separate neighbourhood. In other words, the ghetto system existed. They couldn't touch one another. These people were Tibetan too, but 'different Tibetans, not Mompas'. The Mompas did not consort with them, did not offer them tea if they came home. Even if they did, they didn't reuse the utensils till they had left them outdoors for two or three weeks and purified them with incense. Inter-caste marriages were not practised. Marrying outside your caste meant being expelled from both the caste and society, and being evicted from the village.

But yes, despite the existence of different castes, none of them was an enemy of the Mompas, whose only animosity was towards the Khampas—a wild tribe from the mountains. The lamas had sent them from Tibet to collect taxes. The Mompas were a peaceful race, but the Khampas were wild and cruel. They used to go on a rampage here on the pretext of collecting taxes for their Tibetan masters—there was no limit to their tyranny. Not only did they routinely beat up people, they used to abduct women too, besides taking away gold as well as grains. The Mompas had not always been so poor. It was the Khampas who had robbed them of their riches.

The Chomprung Gompa hadn't exactly come up yesterday—it was four hundred years old. Just as someone named Mera Lama had set up Tawang Gompa, someone named Lama Jung had established Chomprung Gompa. Pemma Ge's family had traditionally provided the priests for the gompa.

Fresh water had not been available in Chomprung earlier. There was a man-eating lake. It was very dangerous, sparing the life of no one who came near it. Lama Jung had made the lake dry up, leaving behind a bare mountain. Then he had arranged for fresh water, creating a new waterfall. He had said, wherever this waterfall flows is where there will be farms, houses, villages, people, prayers.

Lama Pemma Ge chattered merrily, sipping salt tea, while his wife and I drank raksi. I was quite enjoying this. Although I'm not much of a drinker, I was enjoying the raksi here tonight. But I'm not inclined to drink rum or gin or beer or whisky in

Calcutta. Yes, a little dry sherry or dry vermouth before dinner, a chilled Chablis or Hock with the food, or a Beaujolais or Burgundy, and, after the meal, a drop of Cointreau, Cognac, Drambuie, or Creme de Menthe. I have no objection at all to any of this. It's in keeping with the environment abroad, but that's not the case at home. In Calcutta I see many people drinking specifically to get drunk. That's probably why taste is not as important to Bengalis when it comes to alcohol as it is with food. Why not? Because the entire business of drinking is like the forbidden fruit in Bengali life—excluded from everyday domestic habits and external and inimical to middle-class culture. That's probably why it's so crude, so inelegant, so messy in our homes. And so perilous.

But it was different here. It fitted in. I was enjoying it a lot because it was part of daily life, a natural aspect of the environment. I had never visited Santhals the same way, or else I am sure I would have drunk *mohua* and *handia* with them. Sitting in a Calcutta drawing room and guzzling rum or gin or whisky while incisively analysing the kerosene shortage or load shedding or Picasso and Truffaut or Reagan or Thatcher? No, thank you, sir, I have no taste for that.

~

The Land of Draupadi

Suddenly I heard Pemma say, 'My wife is a very good woman. She could have married other men too. One of her sisters has two husbands, and the other one, three. But because Karmo married a lama, she decided not to marry anyone else.'

'What did you say? Two or three husbands?'

'It's not like India. Mompa women can marry more than once. So can the men.'

'If the women marry more than once which of their husbands' houses do they move to?'

'They don't move. The husbands come to the wives' homes. The two husbands live in peace, like brothers. They look after the land, tend to the yaks and cattle.'

'What if there are children? How do they know whose it is?'

'All the children are officially the first husband's. Sometimes brothers marry the same woman if they don't have enough money. The elder brother is the father of all the children. Often, when a husband sees his wife isn't having a baby, but they have a lot of land and cattle and yaks, he personally finds another husband for her so that she can have babies. But those children are officially the first husband's. Sometimes, if he's rich, he acquires another wife too. If the two wives get along, well and good. If not, there's a divorce, there's a case, a fine has to be paid. It can happen with the wife or with the husband.

The richer one will support the other. The one who's in the wrong will pay a fine. There is a panchayat, a village elder too, who decides everything. If a husband runs away, or if a wife abandons her husband, their assets will be distributed between the wife or husband and children, after leaving a little for them. Abandoning your wife or husband is a sin.'

'Love is very popular these days. If it's a love marriage, that's good, it's much cheaper. But if the traditional system is followed, the expenses are higher. The groom's family must pay a dowry for the bride. It can be between two hundred and eight hundred rupees. Five or six large *khada*s and five or six bottles of raksi have to be gifted straightaway. Then if the bride's family accepts the match, there will be feasting, singing and dancing, and a wedding. Lots of raksi will be drunk.'

'So the women get the money?'

'Yes, the women work much harder. They're the ones more sought after. Parents who have no son might sometimes pay a dowry for a son-in-law. But usually it's the bride's family that takes the dowry from the groom's.'

'Do the daughters inherit their parents' property?'

'Both sons and daughters do. Both the parents have their own property.'

'What about the children of women with more than one husband? Whose property do they inherit?'

'All the children get a share of all their fathers' property, of course. What's so complicated?'

'At what age do people get married?'

'Women, between fifteen and twenty or maybe forty; men too, between sixteen and twenty-five or forty.'

I had never heard 'twenty or maybe forty' in the same sentence before. It gave me a great sense of reassurance. Maybe there was still hope. (At least in the land of the Mompas.)

If the marriage was delayed sometimes a baby came earlier. 'This is a matter of shame for the woman.'

'And what about the man?'

'What does the man have to be embarrassed about?' The lama was astonished. His surprise robbed me of a response. That was true. It was the woman who was having a baby. What did it matter to the man!

'And what does the woman do when she's ashamed?'

'She apologizes. That's it. Everything is all right after that. Then she gets married. Whoever marries her becomes the child's father. His property goes to the child.'

How easily Pemma said all this.

If only we could be as logical as the Mompas.

'What does a woman do if her husband dies?'

'She marries again. The children of the first father get his property. The children from the second marriage won't get it.'

'And a man, when his wife dies?'

'The same. He marries again if he can. But it isn't very common unless he's rich. A marriage is expensive.'

'Who are the rich people?'

'Those who have seventy or eighty yaks. Some may have a hundred sheep, or two hundred, and forty or fifty goats. Those are the rich people.'

'And someone with seven or eight yaks, a dozen sheep, and two or three goats?'

'He's rich too. No, medium rich. A yak used to cost two hundred rupees earlier, now the price is fourteen hundred. A sheep cost thirty or forty rupees earlier, but it's two hundred now. A goat too. How can people own too many animals? Most have one or two. And the yaks that come from crossing sheep and yaks, which give the best milk, cost two and a half thousand.'

'Who tends to all this cattle?'

'The children usually take them to graze, and so do the men. The men also cut bamboo, slice wood. What else is there to do? They drink raksi, smoke, knit.'

'Everything else is done by the women?'

'Yes, whether it's working in the fields, weaving cloth on the loom, milking the animals, making butter, brewing chhang and raksi, cooking ... everything. There's no end to Amma's work. That's why a dowry has to be paid for the ammas. They're the ones who matter.'

But the work that identifies the caste is done by the men. For instance, painting thankas, making pottery or things of leather and wood and iron, slaughtering animals and slicing the meat—all this is man's work.

~

Room within a Room

The room we were chatting in was quite a large hall. There was just one door, but no window. A fire was blazing in a fireplace, meaning a clay oven, opposite the door. A lamp too. I saw several thick candles, but they weren't burning. A lantern was lit for me. At once the room was as bright as daylight. Wood fires blazed in the clay ovens, acting as the fireplace. Corn on the cob drying on the floor. Three pans resembling brass pots were simmering on the ovens. The largest was for heating water, the second largest for tea, and the smallest for raksi. There was a rack above the fireplace, something like a mantelpiece, on which lay large, gleaming utensils of brass and copper—pans, small cauldrons, drums, ladles, saucepans. A broom. On one side was a huge *chandoong*, the Tibetan device for making butter tea, made of black wood inlaid with brass and copper plates and studded with beads—which Subhash-babu hadn't let me buy. (He'd been wise.) It had two brass handles too. Opposite the ovens lay two big iron drums with wooden lids, looking exactly like tables. The drums were called *thhirpo*, into which enormous brass ladles (identical to saucepans) were dipped to draw water for cooking and other things. There was no water anywhere else—it was all stored in the room. Everything was in this one room. It had the feel of a tent. There were large wooden trunks against one wall. A black wooden staircase next to the front door led to the mezzanine.

In Pemma Khandu's house, however, this room was not for prayers, but a larder. Since they had an entire gompa, after all. There was a wooden platform too halfway up the wall, on which various things had been put away.

It was nine o'clock by the time we finished chatting and went to bed. They usually ate by seven and went to sleep by eight, waking with the sun at five in the morning. The little girl had not gone to bed either—all of them sat around me, understanding nothing, saying nothing. But they smiled a great deal, and smiles are loquacious.

The sleeping arrangements were fascinating. Large cushions emerged from the big cases stacked along the walls, along with thick blankets and expensive carpets. Laying a few cushions on the floor and spreading a three-thousand-rupee carpet over them, I snuggled cosily beneath a blanket, rolling up my overcoat to use as a pillow. All the lights had been put out. The entire room was dark. The doors were shut. A muted red glow from the extinguished fire danced around the room. The burnt wood was crackling. The sound of breathing. The children had probably fallen asleep. All of them had gone to bed dressed as they were. I did the same. This had been the practice in Tawang too. Like in a train, just take off your shoes and lie down without changing your clothes.

~

Who's There? Who's There?

I was about to drop off when someone suddenly began to bang on the door. Very loudly. Were we being attacked by robbers? Husband and wife both woke up. I lit my torch and they, the lamp. They were very frightened, but after a short conversation with the person outside, their fear seemed to dissipate. It seemed to be someone they knew.

'What is it?'

'A young man. Says the ADC is here to ask after Dr Sen. He's in his car on the main road. Let me take you there. He's asked for you to be taken to him.'

Both husband and wife seemed agitated. The ADC's visit was not a casual affair. I was ready for the road anyway. Slipping on my coat and shoes, I set out.

The ADC? That meant Deuri. At this hour of the night? It was a quarter to ten—midnight in a mountain village. What was the matter?

It was a long climb from the lama's house. A fifteen-minute walk along an uneven, rocky mountain trail. We took a rather unusual route, through someone's farmland, another's yard, and over several high fences and walls (some of which needed ladders to cross), to arrive on the main road. Thankfully I was wearing keds, or else I couldn't have clambered over the fences. The village was fast asleep. Not a light to be seen anywhere. There was only the dim moonlight to guide us. I did have my torch, however, and the young man had one too.

There were three people in the car on the main road—the ADC Mr Deuri, the EAC Mr B. Kumar (who had said with a smile 'I've been in Arunachal for twenty-two years, and only now have I got a decent posting. After all, Tawang is connected by road!'), and the MO Dr Kar, who had given me lunch in his house at Tawang and also lent Dr Lalwani a bedding for my use. One of them was a local from NEFA, one from Uttar Pradesh, and the third, from Orissa. The person they were here to enquire after was from Bengal.

Deuri said, 'I wasn't in Tawang. When I returned I discovered you had left for Chomprung village, that you wanted to live amongst the Mompas. I didn't know you were an anthropologist too. Still, I felt very anxious. For one thing we didn't look after you at all. I hadn't even said goodbye, and now who knew where you had gone? I decided to investigate for myself. These gentlemen wanted to come too. So here we are, all of us. Let me find out where you're staying, how they're treating you.'

What could I say? There could be no adequate response to this concern, this sincerity, this visit after a long and tiring day.

We braved the difficult trail again to return to the lama's house, chatting as we passed through people's courtyards, jumped over apple orchard fences, balanced on the narrow ridges separating potato fields, and walked in the shadow of sleeping houses. The lama had sent the young man on ahead so that his wife could be prepared for the visitors.

The room was resplendent like a god's court when we arrived, looking for all the world like the luxury tent of an Arab sheikh. Lanterns had been lit, carpets and cushions had turned the bedroom into a sitting room. This room changed its character by the minute—now a bedchamber, now a place to entertain. Sunk in a reddish darkness a short while ago, it was a royal hall now. The sleeping Karmo and Kindar had woken up to look after the guests with a smile. They could hardly believe that so many class-one officers were visiting them at home. Having chatted over butter tea and raksi, the guests finally left around eleven-thirty. The young man escorted them to their car. Pemma Khandu wanted to go, too, but they stopped him. Once again the fire was put out and the beds. The visit seemed like a dream now. The room was dark again, with the same reddish glow. The faint smell of extinguished flames, and the occasional crackling of burnt wood.

~

The Birds, They Are A-singing

I woke up to birdsong. The room was empty. Everyone had gone out already. What a lovely morning it was! I went out of the room to the yard outside. The veranda was as large as a courtyard, a wide expanse like a stage, with railings around the periphery. Just below it lay a peach garden. In the distance was a snow-capped mountain range, its lower, forested slopes wrapped in a morning mist like a thin muslin scarf. This scene as soon as I opened my eyes and a whistling bird—a robin magpie, probably—filled my heart at dawn in a way I cannot express.

I remembered Debendranath Tagore. It was this serenity of the Himalayas that had percolated deep into the young Rabindranath's soul.

I was on my way to wash my face after dipping a saucepan (*kiyo*) into the drum of water in the room, when Karmo called out to me and added some hot water. I washed at the railing of the wooden veranda, the water dripping into the peach garden below. Then back into the open with my salt tea. This was a veranda and yard rolled into one. There was a loom on one side. A thick fabric like a warm blanket was being woven on it. Sacks filled with balls of wool lay next to it. The fabric being produced was about a foot wide. All the garments used by the family would be cut and stitched from it. Large vessels of wheat, barley, and corn lay on the veranda, along with enormous gourds and pumpkins. Pots and pans. Umbrellas. They stored all their belongings on the veranda, escaping from the cold inside their room. No one stole other people's things here. The lama said wool had become very expensive, going up from three rupees a kilo to twenty. I didn't spot Chottu anywhere, but Shimpu was sipping tea elegantly from a bowl.

The first task in the morning was to put away the make-shift beds. Then the room turned into a kitchen. One side of the house was probably the mountain itself, for the wall was of rock. The other three walls were made of wood. So was the floor. A small door about five feet in height, with a high door-sill of stone. You had to climb up a stair, and then climb down two on the other side. The room was dark, the eyes adjusting to it gradually. But it was quite warm, since there was no window. There were rafters overhead, smeared with tar. But a room had been added to Pemma Khandu's house, though outside. Constructed recently, it had three or four modern windows with saffron curtains, and three beds inside. I was told three Tibetan lamas were visiting, and it was for them that the room had been built. They had been guests there for several months now. They didn't come into the house, so far as I could see.

The family was done with cooking and breakfast soon after waking up. By seven, everyone had eaten their fill of rice, paa, tea, and fried eggs and gone off to work. Then began Amma's household work, helped by her daughter. Several women arrived to work in the peach garden. The women here smoked, but not the lamas. No one in this family did.

'Mompas don't have ganja or bhang,' the lama said. 'Just tobacco, snuff, and raksi. Sometimes also *araa*, *lopani*, sing chhang, or chhang.' Pemma Ge's wife was really hardwork-ing. Winnowing barley and wheat, putting it out to dry, packing it away in sacks. The lama had left for the gompa in the morning. I went out for a stroll. Tinkling sounds— here too, a pair of young boys were out with a herd of yaks. Apparently, they wept inconsolably when a yak died, for it's the loved members of the family who are reborn as yaks. The yak is Goddess Lakshmi.

The lama's wife was gathering the grain in a beautifully polished copper- and brass-plated measuring vessel. I'd have taken one home if it were available. I'd also have taken the bowls in which tea was served. They drank their tea in gleaming, polished wooden bowls, shaped like Danish containers. They ate their food in bowls with tiny stands and lids. Why lids? So that the food did not turn cold.

The primary difference with the mornings in Tawang was that birds sang in the woods here. There were large trees and birds here, both of which were missing in Tawang. It might be the same mountain range, but the difference in altitude had changed the nature of the place.

Pemma would return now. I'd better go and see what the gompa looked like in daylight. Urakin had gone to school, where she studied in class three. The ani was preparing to return to her ani gompa. Karmo was working in the orchard with her eldest daughter. At one point, she brought me some peaches from the garden, wrapped in leaves. Raw and succulent red-and-green peaches. Very tasty with a pinch of salt. I put some in my bags for my daughters. They had never seen raw peaches. Pemma would return with me after my visit to the gompa.

It was as I'd thought—the tantric gods and goddesses looked far less fearsome by day.

Meanwhile, a neighbour arrived with a gift of three eggs and a khada. Then came Amma's two beautiful sisters, one of whom had her grandson strapped to her back. Her son and daughter-in-law had gone out on work. This was the sister with two husbands. The other sister was holding her four- or five-year-old granddaughter by the hand. Both the children were very sweet. The granddaughter even had something like a cowbell attached to her waist. She offered a namaste when asked, followed by a salaam when told, and hid behind her grandmother at once with a smile. So she was the one with three husbands? Certainly a beauty! Both of them were over sixty, but they didn't look a day above forty. Clearly there were shades of Shangri-La here. They too had brought khadas and five eggs each, for a guest at their sister's house had to be welcomed warmly, after all. I left the eggs for the family and packed the khadas. A khada was similar to a faded white *gamchha* made with a very thin starched gauze of the kind used for bandages, which was used in Tibet instead of a garland. Cheesecloth looked exactly like this in England. Whether it was a god or a human, their way of showing respect was to offer a khada. The eggs too. Just as we offer sweets and garlands.

I was seeing polygamous but morally upright women for the first time in my life. Unfortunately I couldn't ask them any questions because of the language gap. Not every conversation could take place using the lama's services as an interpreter. Soon the guests joined Karmo at work in the garden. These people never remained idle, not even when visiting someone. No wonder they were so beautiful.

~

In Every Life, in Every Generation, Endlessly

'Would you like to see the place? Maybe visit the villages nearby?' Pemma Ge asked me. 'Since you're so keen to meet lamas, let me take you to see Lama Choche Rimpo Che. An authentic Tibetan lama. Even if he's not as high up as the Dalai Lama or the Panchen Lama, he's still a very important lama. These lamas remember a great deal from their past lives. He came here with the Dalai Lama in 1959. Many of them are born with the ability to read old manuscripts. Some even have signs from their previous lives. He has a birthmark like that. He can tell the future miraculously. We can meet Rimpo Che if we go now. You can walk, can't you? Or should I get the horse?'

'What? You have a horse? You didn't show me. Is it a long way?' There was a small field in front of the gompa, surrounded by pine forests. A beautiful, compact brown horse was grazing in the field. I saw Chottu the dog playing there too.

'That's my horse,' Pemma said with a shy smile. It wasn't very far. I didn't need a horse. We walked to one side of the mountain, near the slope. The edge of a village. I didn't know whether this was still Chomprung or some other village. There were several fences that had to be crossed, some yards too. Some footwork, some leap-work. I quickly realized why

Mr Kumar had said Tawang was a good posting because it was well-connected by roads. And this was not even a wild mountainous area, but tamed, civilized human habitation.

A bungalow. A man working in the field in front of it said he would find out whether the lama would meet us. We waited in the yard. There was a tall wooden post, with a tiny wooden cage on top, complete with a little veranda in front of it. We found a monkey sitting there. It came down on spotting us, perhaps in the hope of some food. But we had nothing to offer it.

It climbed back up and, having got hold of a broken mirror from somewhere, lay down on its back to examine its own face, which wore a rather mournful expression. There was a thin chain around the monkey's ankle. If only we had some food to give it. Poor thing!

Some people had gathered around me in the meantime. Pemma Ge asked them, 'Can you give us any food for the monkey?' A little boy ran off.

'It's a she-monkey,' the lama informed me. 'The monkeys had come in a bunch to steal corn. When they were chased away, her mother left her behind and ran off. Lama Rimpo adopted her and brings her up like a daughter.' The chained monkey was busy scanning her own face in the broken mirror.

It felt like a perfect reflection of our internal life. This was a potent image from poetry. This was just what human life was.

The little boy returned soon, having got hold of some peanuts and popcorn. The monkey climbed down to pick out the nuts and eat them before going back to her cage and picking up the mirror.

The man had brought us some news. His face alight with happiness, Pemma Ge said, 'Come, Rimpo Che is asking for us. Don't forget to find out what your future holds.' I had shared my life story already. Pemma Khandu and Karmo

wanted that either I should reconcile with my husband immediately, or I should get married, also immediately. It wasn't
right to wander around alone like this. None of us had enough
of the language to explain or to understand that, far from wandering around alone, I was in my nest incubating my eggs.
The lama's Hindi was as spectacular as mine. Who was going
to claim the upper hand? But the trouble began when we were
ushered into Rimpo Che's presence.

These were reincarnated lamas. The Dalai Lama's aides
sought them out from their homes in Tibet, after he revealed
which lama would be reincarnated next, in which village, and
in whose family. The child would have a specific birthmark.
Reincarnated Tibetan lamas belonged to the highest class, and
were the most respected. They read manuscripts constantly,
remaining engrossed in spiritual discussions about good and
evil, reincarnation and pre-incarnation, sins and virtues, the
past and the future, the soul and the maker. Once, a Dalai
Lama had apparently been born near Tawang, next to a gompa
named Urgiling. A camphor tree stood there. The lamas of
Tibet had learnt this in their dream, and had sent emissaries to
Urgiling to take the child to them. The Urgiling Gompa and
the ancient camphor tree were still in existence. I could even
pay a visit if I had enough time, for you could go in a jeep.

Tantra is an essential aspect of the Buddhist faith, where the
role of the woman is not minor at all. Tantric goddesses like
Lokeshwari, Tara, Mahakali, and Kali rule with great authority
and infinite grace. Yama himself was their male companion.
My friend Sanjukta would have found this trip far more useful
than I did—she was researching Tantra in the Netherlands.
Each of the gompas here had an abundance of manuscripts and
many ancient paintings on thankas. There were myths, folklore, and legends passed on by word of mouth. I felt a strong

desire to collate the myths, but there was no time. I have thought of going back one day. But five years have passed. Just as the legend of how Jung Lama brought water to Chomprung was like the story of King Sagar's sons and Bhagirath, an archetypal story, so was the one about how Tawang got its name, and four or five other explanations and narratives ... the fact was that thousands of stories were floating here in the air like cotton balls. You just had to catch them. But I was not only a beggar when it came to the language but also poverty-stricken in terms of time—and so my bag of stories remained unfilled.

Pemma Ge said with great reverence, 'He is a very important lama. His name is Choche Rimpo Che. He's forty-six, and he comes from the best-known gompa in Tibet. He has a birthmark on his arm, which is how the Dalai Lama's emissaries located him and took him from his family. He too remembers his past life in entirety, his own gompa. He has recounted the details of the gompa's assets, as well as the names of his parents in his previous life. Not a surprise, for reincarnated lamas can do this. He is a very honest man. He has left so many golden figures of Buddha, so many golden idols of the gods and goddesses, back in Tibet to come here. He lives here like an impoverished man, visiting the poor and helpless all the time. He has no personal ambition. He is already very learned, and he keeps studying more. Compassion incarnate. He has adopted many animals. This is his twelfth life. He has memories of all his previous eleven lives. He can tell you the entire history.'

His compassion was beyond doubt. Two dogs in the veranda began to bark furiously as we were on our way to his room. They had to be chained eventually. Inside the temple we found another pampered dog sharing a mat with the lama, leaning against his cushion and playing languorously on the carpet.

Who knew what sort of creatures they had been in their previous births? A fourth tiny, furry object climbed into my lap. It was difficult to gauge the lama's age from his ascetic appearance. He was not as portly as Pemma. He said a great many things, speaking slowly and gravely. But Pemma did not have the ability to translate any of this into Hindi. Therefore, it was not possible to have much of a conversation with the lama. He spoke only to Pemma. Although Pemma reminded me many times to ask about my future, I could not bring myself to do it. I won't claim I had no desire to know, but I simply couldn't bring up this most personal of things. My ego came in the way. So I had my pride too? In other words, I was not free. 'All pride is bondage. The pride of one's own grief is a powerful chain.' I remained silent. Pemma pointed out the birthmark signifying the lama's previous life. A red mole on his right arm.

The lama treated us with great solicitousness to salt tea and biscuits served in Japanese crockery. As we were leaving, I saw a beautiful horse, bursting with health, grazing in front of his house.

'Look, he has a horse just like yours.'

'How can you say that?' Pemma said in embarrassment. 'Do you suppose he has just one horse? He has seven. He bought three himself, and the villagers gifted him the other four.'

'What will he do with seven? Is he the Sun God? Or does he ride a different one each day of the week?'

'No, people have gifted him the horses, that's all.'

Seven horses, four canines, one monkey, and several villages full of trusting people—irrespective of what his past lives were like, this one was clearly going well for Rimpo Che. But not being able to understand the language was agonizing.

~

Breakfast Is Ready

Spinning the 'mani' wheel once more and thinking of god, I followed Pemma Ge into the house. It was noon. Amma also abandoned the garden to return and light the clay oven. Time to make lunch.

A couple of young boys and girls, not part of the family, arrived, one of them sprawling on the floor with a plateful of fluffy toasted corn pieces (what my daughters call popcorn) to eat. Amma took an enormous gourd and brandished a dagger before slicing it. The food was ready soon. Something like what you'd get if you kneaded some flour and then boiled the dough instead of making rotis with it (which I was told was made of millet, instead of rice), paa, butter tea, and raksi. Raksi even in the afternoon. I'd never seen anyone in this house drink chhang.

'Meals like these aren't made every afternoon though. When someone takes the cattle out to graze or to farm on distant fields, they just take some tiffin along.'

'What sort of tiffin?'

'Why, momos stuffed with yak meat, or a chutney of jhyan and chillies.'

'When do they return?'

'In the evening. Then they drink their tea, followed by raksi. They rest a bit. Dinner is served at seven. Some more raksi after dinner, and then prayers. Bed by eight. The lamas have a slightly different routine, though. No raksi.'

What did Amma and her family do from the time they got up in the morning? First, clear out the makeshift beds and put them away, sweep the floor, and then light the oven.

Heat the water.

Have a wash.

Make tea.

Make the vegetables, the jhyan, the paa.

Go out after a meal. Look after the farming, take care of the yaks and goats. The men went off to slice bamboo, cut and fetch wood, make planks, and take the cattle out to graze. When Amma returned from her work in the field she wove wool on the loom—and also knitted sweaters and caps and socks and mufflers with knitting needles. She threshed the barley and wheat and set it out to dry. Sometimes she made raksi or chilli pickle or yak milk butter. She made meat jerky, putting everything away in tins. Amma had so much to do. The ammas of this world never run out of work. No wonder one has to pay dowry to their parents to bring them home.

Bathing was not part of their routine. Just once a year. In spring.

These people were very reticent. I didn't see them talking among themselves either. They were quiet in general. All they did was smile. When they did speak, it was in low voices.

~

The Picture-maker

After lunch Pemma Khandu and I went off to explore the village. Pemma said, 'Let me show you thankas being painted.' Over on the other side was where 'someone from the tribe of painters' lives.

I spun the mani on my way out. *Om mani padme hum.*

Going past his gompa, and then a potato field, we entered the compound of someone's house. A huge vegetable garden. The house was situated deeper within the premises. We ran across a girl of fourteen or fifteen on our way. An angelic child of three or four was dancing alongside, holding her hand. Pemma had a conversation with her. She answered with a smile, greeting me, and then left. Pemma said, 'He's home. This was the painting-maker's wife, and that was their son.'

'Such a young wife? And she has such a big boy? How old is she?'

'Nineteen or twenty.'

'And the one who paints?'

'Twenty-one or twenty-two.'

The room downstairs was unlocked. The door was wide open. There was no one there. Kitchen utensils were arranged neatly; the teapot was on the oven.

Pemma went up the narrow flight of stairs to the first floor. I waited downstairs.

It was a similar room, except that the veranda in front was narrow and had a thatched roof. In front lay the vegetable garden. The mountain was in the distance. Pemma came back to escort me upstairs. It was just like the prayer room in Yeshiani's house. Small, but very well-lit, with a huge window. Arrangements for prayers on one side. A silver bowl filled with water in front of a figure of the Buddha on a wooden platform. Several thankas of gods and goddesses were hanging on the walls, while lamps and incense sticks were burning.

An old man sat there, reading aloud from a manuscript in a lilting tone. A beautiful scene. He greeted me.

Next to him, facing the window, sat a young man, sideways from the gods and goddesses, painting intently. Several bowls of earthen pigments lay on a large brass plate in front of him. Putting his brush down, he greeted me with a shy smile.

He was making two paintings at the same time, adding blue to both at the moment. Patches of blue were emerging. One of the paintings was of Mahakali, and the other, of Gautama Buddha. I thought they were very beautiful. How much? Forty rupees, Pemma told me after finding out. I wanted to pay at once, but Lou Chhong (the artist) didn't accept my offer. 'Place your order,' he said, 'I'll paint it later. These have been ordered already by the Arts and Crafts Centre.' (They sold these thankas at a hundred and fifty rupees there; didn't Lou Chhong know this?) There wasn't a trace of Camel colours here.

Pemma informed me that Lou Chhong's father Tundrila was an old man now and could no longer wield the paintbrush, which was why he devoted his time to prayers and reading the scriptures. Lou Chhong was a worthy son, who supported his father with his earnings, and took care of his wife and child's needs too. His mother was dead. Lou Chhong's father had run the household with his earnings from painting, and he was doing the same. He insisted on getting tea for us, but I didn't want to interrupt his work. We left. It was time to go back.

~

A Hundred Miles, a Hundred Miles

I was supposed to wait with my luggage at the point where the ADC's jeep had stopped. I said goodbye to the lama and his family over and over again, taking their hands in mine. I had no riches in my city-made basket, in my 'box of bombast', to pay them back adequately for so much kindness, which had touched my heart even without having a language in common.

Urakin Khamo pranced all the way to the main road behind us, while Karmo and Kindar bade us farewell from their doorstep.

They too had given me khadas and fruit for the journey.

As we waited at the head of the road, many people came up to Pemma to ask what the matter was, why was his guest leaving so soon? Was she not going to stay nine or ten months like those three Tibetan lamas?

Shattering the quiet, calm mountain afternoon with its horn, a truck arrived suddenly. No bus was available, we would have to travel by truck.

Subhash-babu jumped out.

'Where's the luggage? I thought you were going to become a monk and go off to Ani Gompa.

'If only I were so lucky. Where's the puppy? Did you forget?

'If only I were so lucky. No chance of forgetting. Everyone from the ADC, the EAC, and the MO to the ADC's driver has been reminding me. We mustn't forget Dr Sen's puppy. I don't know why you people have to make these short visits, Madam, and make us miss you afterwards. Get in now, we're late....'

'Where, where's my puppy?'

'Which one?'

'Meaning?'

'I've got two. One's a Lhasa Apso. Those are the ones people buy. No one's seen a Tibetan hound in civilized areas. They're meant to guard yaks. Here they guard government offices. That's how you came to know of them.'

'Lhasa Apsos are those stubby, fluffy, short-legged ones? I don't like those. They have no self-confidence, always bad-tempered. They try to bite. I don't care for cat-like dogs. Cats should be like cats, and dogs, like dogs.'

'That's very good news. They wanted to keep the other one—they can take it to the plains and sell it for four hundred rupees. Although they're claiming they will keep it as a pet.'

'Who's they?'

'There's a driver of ours in this truck, travelling with his family on holiday. He'll take one of the pups. You have first choice.'

'I'll take mine.'

Someone tossed a soft, warm, tender ball of wool into my arms from the truck. I got into the truck holding him. He licked my hand with his tiny tongue and gazed at my face with his kohl-lined eyes. Behind me lay the man-eating lake and life-giving waterfall of Chomprung Gompa, Lou Chhong and his paintbrushes, Pemma Khandu and his ripe-peach-like wife. The village was obliterated like a dream by the dust raised by the truck. Around the corner loomed a forest.

~

Twilight in the Afternoon

I had dozed off. Subhash-babu said, 'Look behind you. Someone's bidding you farewell.'

Turning, I saw a magical sight. Tawang Gompa was flashing like a crown in the sunlight, high up over the head of the wooded hillside. Suddenly I felt a pang of sadness. Goodbye forever in this lifetime, Tawang. Another part of my heart said, which of these is yours, traveller?

The truck was going downhill. There were clumps of small trees by the road. 'All of these are rhododendron copses. When they bloom, you know, the colours will drive you mad.'

'Trees so small?'

'That's what this variety is like, very short.'

At another turn in the road Subhash-babu shouted out again, 'Take a look. The last and final view. You won't see Tawang Gompa anymore. The last time.'

This time it was even farther away. One more afternoon was ending. The light was the colour of the setting sun, and Tawang Gompa seemed to be made of copper.

This time the view made me even sadder. Two mountains away now. Still regal. Tawang was receding into the distance, becoming unreal. Soon it would become a dream for the night.

~

Hindi Chini Bhai Bhai

'This waterfall, you know, had turned red during the war. A river of blood. A little lower, next to the dam, there was a wall of bodies of dead soldiers. The time we went through, my god!'

Villages lay as serene as a painting on the green slopes. Villages and, with them, waterfalls, streams, and wooden bridges. I hadn't spotted any of these on the way in; it had been dark then.

'We'll take the road past Rupa.'

'Rupa? What a lovely name.'

'A lovely name and a lovely town too. Our Morarji Desai is coming there. He'll fly in, though.'

'Did the Chinese soldiers capture these areas?'

'Of course! They went down all the way to Bomdila, didn't they? But you know what, if the Chinese came back the villagers would welcome them with open arms.'

'What do you mean? Didn't you say they had made the blood flow like a river?'

'They didn't kill civilians. They behaved in exemplary fashion with the villagers. The first thing they did was loot the mint, and then distribute the money in sackfuls in the villages. That was it, they had purchased the poor.'

The other gentleman, our third passenger, spoke now. 'Not just money, but rations too. They distributed rations as soon as they entered. They even gave away their own military rations.'

'And the way they treated the women? That was worthy of example too. They didn't trouble a single woman.'

'As for our soldiers, the less said the better.'

'This sounds like the Second World War. The Japanese enemy comes into India, winning the hearts of the people of Manipur with model behaviour, while the people are driven to anger by the havoc unleashed by patriotic INA troops....'

'What about the Bangladesh War?'

'But even if that was the case, we can't say it. We'll be called anti-nationals. Scoundrels!'

On the way up I had seen the wreckage of a small plane on the road to Nuruanang. Nobody knew whether it was from 1942 or 1962. It looked shiny and new. Who knew whom it had belonged to?

~

Dwa Suparna

The road changed its appearance continuously. Near Rupa it bifurcated into two. They didn't let us turn towards Rupa—preparations were underway for Morarji Desai's arrival.

'Can't we make a quick trip? Take a look? We'll come back this way.' After much cajoling the military police agreed for some reason and took down the car number with a smile. 'Come back soon, mind.' All this just for me to get a glimpse of Rupa. The others had been there many times.

The truck made a trip up and down the main road of Rupa. Then we took the road to Dirang. The vehicle had been allotted exclusively to us, so we could go wherever we liked. If this had been a ration truck, there would have been no chance of detours.

Bumla Tawang was asleep on my lap, growling to get rid of demons from his nightmares. I had named him Bumla Tawang. I didn't get to see Bum-La. An enchanted memory of a quick glimpse and then nothing—let it remain locked in that state. Of getting a little and wanting more.

'We'll spend the night at Dirangjong. Rooms have been booked at IB. One for the men, one for the women. That is to say, the driver Hari's wife and child and Dr Sen. I am certain Dr Sen will have no problems anywhere in the world, but Bihurani might, thrown in suddenly with a doctorate....'

'Bihurani? Is she from Assam?'

'Uh-huh. The driver is a Bihari who's married a Bengali. A Bengali bride with an Assamese name, Bihurani.

'A Bengali bride with an Assamese name and a Bihari husband? How lovely!'

'And a Tibetan dog.'

'Where are they?'

'Here, in this very truck, in the back.'

Our road ran past a stream, but in the distance, we could see the bank of another beautiful river. 'What place is that? What a wide and fast-flowing river....'

'That's the Dirang.'

'They have such Sanskritic names. Everything ends with an *ang* sound—Tawang, Kamang, Dirang, Jang, Chomprung. Do these names have any meaning or are they just sounds?'

'Of course they have meanings. The word Tawang itself has three meanings—*Ta* meaning horse, and *Wam*, meaning where horses can be taken care of well, a stable, that is.'

'A second meaning is that the gods descended from the Ta to give them the boon of *Ang*, that is, they got off their horses to bless them, and so *Ta-ang*.'

'And the third meaning is that the tantric god Tadrin, who was here on a holiday, was so pleased with the way the Mompas took care of him that he gave them a boon to alleviate their misery. What boon? The horse. They didn't have horses here earlier. Since then the place has been named *Ta-ong*; in other words, a boon in the form of a horse.'

'I get it, a figure of speech. Now tell me what Dirang means. Why that name?'

'Dirang? Dirang is named for the river. It's next to the Dirang River, you see.'

'Why is the Dirang River named Dirang, for that matter?'

'Dirang means two birds.'

'Two birds? What a beautiful name!'

Dwa Suparna?

One bird pecks at the food, while the other only looks on.

One consumes, the other abstains.

The Dirang was as powerful as it is pretty.

The swiftness in the mountain and the breadth in the valley—it had captured both. Dirang wasn't an incorrect name.

Don't I have two birds like these within me? The same two birds…?

One a torrent, the other a pool?

One just gathers pebbles, just gathers leaves. The other breaks the rudder, tears the sails, and unmoors the boat.

One holds on tight, the other lets go.

I'm getting to know
The one I've let go of.
Now that I have moved away I can see
my long-known world of joys and sorrows
And with it
What lies beyond, the untraceable.

Bumla Tawang, lying in my lap and dreaming, growled to ask, 'You haven't really learnt to let go, have you?'

You keep holding on tighter.

Have you really been able to let go of Tawang?

~

About the Author and the Translator

NABANEETA DEV SEN is one of the most versatile Indian writers in Bengali today. Her unique style of expression, varied experience of life, and a rare sense of humour are evident in her vast literary output. She has written in many genres, including poems, plays, short stories, novels, columns, belles-lettres, travelogues, memoirs, and critical essays. She is also a hugely acclaimed writer for children. She was a professor of comparative literature at Jadavpur University, Kolkata, India. Among her many awards are Mahadevi Verma National Award (1992), Sahitya Akademi Award (1999), Padmashree (2000), Gopichand National Literary Award (2016), Kalinga Literary Award (2017), and Big Little Book Award (2017). Some of her well-known works are *Naba-Neeta* (1996), *Sita Theke Shuru* (1996), *Bama-bodhini* (1997), and *Tumi Manasthir Karo* (2009).

ARUNAVA SINHA translates classic, modern, and contemporary Bengali fiction and non-fiction into English. His translations have been published in India, the UK, and the USA in English, and in several European and Asian countries through further translation. Twice the winner of the Crossword translation award, for Sankar's *Chowringhee* (2007) and Anita Agnihotri's *Seventeen* (2011), and the winner of the Muse India Translation Award for Buddhadeva Bose's *When the Time Is Right* (2013), he has also been shortlisted for the Independent Foreign Fiction Prize for his translation of *Chowringhee* (2009).